Praise for
I'm Not Here

"In the memoir *I'm Not Here*, as a young Jerry Vis is trying to run away from a religious 1950's boarding school, he has a powerful experience he's not even sure is real: A laconic mountain man, skinning a bear, tells him, "Thou art of scant use to thyself." Vis takes this to mean he should be true to himself, which becomes a guiding light for the teenager. By turns deeply moving and hilarious, *I'm Not Here* immerses the reader in Vis's thoroughly human attempts to make sense of life, faith, friendship, romance... and his dysfunctional family."

—**Roberto Loiederman**, co-author of *The Eagle Mutiny*, a nonfiction account of the only mutiny on an US ship in modern times.

"In the tradition of classics like *Catcher in the Rye* and *To Kill A Mockingbird*, Jerry Vis' *I'm Not Here* takes us on a journey through our own youth seen through the lens of acquired wisdom. With great wit and care, we are invited to remember what we thought we knew about growing up. From our first questions about religion to the awkward dawn of our budding sexuality, no one can escape the unwelcome realization that our families just may be the reason we're all crazy."

—**Stephen Kellogg**, musician and author of *Objects In the Mirror: Thoughts on a Perfect Life from an Imperfect Person.*

"For those of us who've gone through life feeling different, *I'm Not Here,* is a must read. Jerry Vis' experiences will make you laugh and touch your heart. It's a delightfully entertaining read of adventures, both real and imagined."

—**Anne Carlucci**, Film Producer, *Who Killed JonBenét?*

I'm Not Here

Strange Relatives, a Stranger Boarding School, and the Saving Grace of Art and Love

JERRY VIS

RIVERCLIFF
BOOKS & MEDIA

Copyright ©2022 by Jerry Vis

Rivercliff Books & Media

www.rivercliffbooks.com

Cover design by Valentina Pinova
Birdcage drawing by Jerry Vis
Edited by Carol Stanley

ISBN: 978-1-954566-03-3

All Rights Reserved

Publisher's Cataloging-in-Publication data

Names: Vis, Jerry, author.
Title: I'm not here : strange relatives , a stranger boarding school , and the saving grace of art and love / Jerry Vis.
Description: Boulder, CO: Rivercliff Books & Media, 2022.
Identifiers: LCCN 2022932657 | ISBN 978-1-954566-03-3 (paperback) | 978-1-954566-04-0 (ebook)
Subjects: LCSH Vis, Jerry--Childhood and youth. | Vis, Jerry--Family. | Boarding school students--Anecdotes. | Boarding schools--United States--Anecdotes. | Boarding schools--Virginia--Anecdotes. | Christian education--Virginia--Anecdotes. | Southern States--Social life and customs--21st century. | BISAC BIOGRAPHY & AUTOBIOGRAPHY / Personal Memoirs
Classification: LCC LC47 .V57 2022 | DDC 373.222--dc23

For Benjamin.

My son, Benjamin, presented me with an Apple® laptop a number of years ago. I stared at the thing and asked, "What's that for?" His response was, "I thought you might want to write down some of your stories."

Contents

Introduction 9
1. Coming in on a Wing and a Prayer 12
2. Disorientation 23
3. Thinks Again 34
4. Goin' Home, Goin' Home, Lord I'm Goin' Home 43
5. There's No Place Like Home for the Holidays 50
6. The Lord Giveth and the Lord Taketh Away 59
7. Burma Shave 71
8. He's Bad News 80
9. Oh Shenandoah, I Hear Ya Callin' 95
10. The Get Away 105
11. Yeah, Right 119
12. Westward-Ho! 136
13. An Opposing Opined Opinion 154
14. Addicted to Bad Behavior 158
15. Hope Springs a Leak 164
16. A Little Bird Told Me 175
17. It's a Lou-Lou 181
18. Heart and Soul 188
19. Progress I Could Live With 199
20. The Natural State of Being: Complete Randomness? 204
21. Oh, Dear, What Can the Matter Be? 210
22. And Your Name, Sir, Is What? 223
Epilogue 233
About the Author 234

Introduction

Learning to Think Sideways

When I was seven years old, learning to cross streets, I was told to look left, then right, then back again to the left. My friend Buddy—he lived upstairs—forgot, and I saw him struck by a car as I watched from my living room window in 1946. Years later, I was guilty of the same thing—not looking both ways—except it had to do with a place, its people, and the way they thought. It was implied at that time that there was nothing unique in that. After all, I was a don't-tell-me-what-to-do teenager.

As of this writing, it has been seventy-four years since I began that trip across that youthful street. At that time, I was angry, and frightened, confused, almost terminally so. As a result, challenges came stalking me from behind, forcing me to live in a perpetual state of ambiguity with some issues unresolved even to this day. For years I told myself it didn't matter. But now it does. Thinking about it, talking about it for these many years hasn't quite resolved the lingering questions. I began to write, haltingly in fading pencil, in spiral note pads over a twenty-year period, until this moment when it became imperative to finish. But why and for whom?

With that in mind, I've asked myself, multiple times, why would anyone of the seven plus billion narcissists on this planet be more interested in what I might have to say than what they might have to say? Ultimately, I understood it didn't matter. I wrote for myself. Never thought or expected it to go further than scribblings forgotten in a box in the attic. Thus far, not even my dear children have shown any interest in reading what I've written. Which is a good argument for getting rid of all electronic handheld devices or looking for a new family. But now, here you and I are staring at each other across these pages.

Finally, I wrote from necessity to understand what happened and how it affected my life. And though I would never have believed it then, it changed my life in both painful and positive ways no one then could have imagined, including myself.

In 1951, I was a happy kid living in Paterson, N.J., with lots of friends, a secure home, loving mother, newly acquired freedom to go off on my own, ride my bike in the street, go to the movies, etc., etc., etc. A year later, my father, a recent "born-again" Christian, shunted me off to a religious boarding school in rural Virginia, with kids who talked funny and thought I was sinful beyond hope because I lived so close to New York City. I was buried under a heap of rules burdensome enough to collapse a packhorse. And as far as I could tell, I was the only one bothered by it. What was most difficult during those teenage years was that it didn't matter how many times I looked both ways. The unexpected always ran me over.

These, then, are not stories of a great heroic effort, or of surviving against all odds. There was no overt abuse, no external trauma like a war. Just people missing each other in a dark fog born of an inability to imagine that anything but their own answer could be the right one.

Isn't life a curious thing, though? We start off on the young side of twenty, thinking there's a poetic rhyme and reason to life. But for most of the time beyond that age, it's a struggle just to achieve impersonal prosaic prose. My dilemma then, I suspect, was how to deal with an ethos devoted to a numbing view of life. But did I have that right? If I did, then wasn't it simply a matter of looking left for that second time to stay alive? It wasn't that simple.

Until the age of eleven, I had an uneventful, blue-collar, stickball-in-the-street childhood in Paterson, N.J. My father was no more than a vaporous, bring-home-the-bacon presence. Then he got religion. I thought of it as a virulent infection –yes, even at the age of eleven—which he was bound and determined to inflict on all he knew. It started with my mother and myself and, for reasons that will become clear in the following story, it altered her life and mine forever.

1

COMING IN ON A WING AND A PRAYER

AUGUST 1952 · 12 YEARS OLD

It was a dark and stormy night as the Enola Gay lifted off the runway at the Caldwell Airfield on its third historic meeting with destiny. No, no, no. Too simple.

There was a severe storm the night the Enola Gay, lifted off the runway at the Caldwell Airfield on its third historic meeting with destiny.

I wasn't satisfied. It needed more oomph for a "What If" Story. As an only child, I habitually talked to myself.

"Jerry?" a summoning call from my mother. I pretended I didn't hear.

"Let's start over," I said to myself. The "let's" word was, of course, me, talking to the "other" me.

The night sky darkened, and the stars twinkled out as storm clouds began to cover the golden twilight just as the Enola Gay lifted off the runway at the Caldwell Airfield into an approaching severe storm, on its third historic meeting with destiny.

"That's worse. I don't like this either," I whispered under my breath.

"Yeah, you're right," came an agreeable, Other-Me response.

These made-up stories were usually instigated by some weirdness that occurred, or that I heard about, or I didn't like,

like my sixth-grade teacher, Miss Sickles, at PS 12. For a while, my friend Dennis and I made them up together before we fell afoul of the law and his mother. We had started to act out the stories. In the case of Miss Sickles, we actually shot the wrong teacher with our pea shooters and wound up getting involved with the police. What-If-Stories we called them. I hadn't made one up for quite a while, but my serious, desperate, disagreeable, fast approaching, terrible situation called for one immediately. The problem? These stories often took on a life of their own, as if there was a secret agreement between me, the storyteller, and some perverse hidden part of me that shanghaied the tale to lead me on a merry chase.

My mother called again from the kitchen, "Jerry, I need you to set the table for supper."

"Yeah, I just need to finish something, Mom." *Well, at least she didn't ask about that stupid questionnaire.*

The freshly painted Enola Gay stood out crisply against the setting sun as the determined pilot willed the super-fortress bomber to climb above an on-coming hurricane. That's better. I like this.

It was in the Paterson Evening News *that the Enola Gay was going to fly south from the Caldwell Airfield at the end of the week. I knew immediately that this was my one and only best chance to solve my dilemma. But that meant I would need to sneak on board the plane and hide in the rear gun turret before...*

"Jerry," (please God, not the questionnaire) "have you finished that questionnaire for the school in Virginia? Your father will be home from work soon, and the first thing he'll wanna do is see it."

I didn't respond.

I had just completed the Strombecker wooden model kit of the B-29 bomber of the Enola Gay used in the atomic bombing of Hiroshima, and the last of the World War II models I needed to complete the set of warplanes suspended from my bedroom ceiling—which they shared with my super day glow stars.

"Jerry?"

"Yes, Mom." Ugh.

"Is it done?"

"Is what done?"

"That questionnaire."

"No, not yet."

"You've only got a half-hour. Do that now. I'll set the table."

I was looking through my desk drawer for an eye hook and some nylon fishing line to hang the B-29 among my other planes. I didn't think the Enola Gay had ever been used for anything after its bombing run over Japan. The second of the three meetings with destiny was known only to me and a few friends. Thanks to Mrs. Levy's geography lesson in fifth-grade, I had the plane pick up and carry my hometown of Paterson to an Iowa (or was it Nebraska?) cornfield so it could be the second-largest city in that state, a step up from third place in New Jersey. The next appointment with destiny was my hijacking of the plane to fly me far away: anything to avoid going to Shenandoah Valley Academy in three weeks. The paperwork my mother asked about had been lost in the chaos atop my desk for weeks and was now spattered with the paint I had used to finish the Enola Gay.

The top of the questionnaire simply asked for name, address, age, and sex. The next part wasn't too bad. Where do you attend church? How many years? Born or converted to the gospel of Christ? Are you a non-member of the Seventh Day Adventist Church? How did you hear about our school? Plus ten more questions. And then the next part: write a two hundred fifty-word essay on why you want to attend Shenandoah Valley Academy. My honest opinion could be stated in five words: I-*don't*-want-to-go! Which is what I wrote on the form.

I was standing on my desk chair with my back to the door, adjusting the dramatic angle of the suspended Enola Gay bomber, when my father entered the room. I froze as if I were glued to the Enola Gay with Duco Cement.

"Have you finished the essay?

Silence...

"NO?!" he assumed. "Why not?"

I heard him rummage around my desk for the questionnaire.

"What's this you wrote, 'I-don't-want-to-go?'"

There was a slight lull, which seemed to last for several weeks while I remained, arms over my head, back to my father, stuck to the Enola Gay in a position that must have looked like surrender.

"Oh Jerry, you must go. Must. It's God's will." His tone was now contrived and mellifluous. He had been trying all summer to sell me on the idea. He had gone from a dictatorial, "it's God's will," to this over-the-top sugary "it's God's will," followed by a forced smile. It made our confrontations easier, but it never changed the direction of the issue: only father knows best.

I never became belligerent or hostile, just completely depressed. If I had been sentenced to life imprisonment for a crime I'd not committed, I couldn't have been more dismal. But as I learned, dismal doesn't cut it with God. Maybe with the Devil, but not God, and certainly not with his handyman, my father.

My father had been saying 'God's will' now for two years since he nearly killed himself with alcohol and then got religion. He said it so often that it had morphed into a single word: *Godswill*. It was now his habitual response to every intrusive or unpleasant thing that anyone other than himself encountered. Your dog died? Godswill. You have to sit in the corner for an hour? Godswill. Your best friend just moved out of state? Godswill. At this point in my life, being sent to boarding school was also Godswill, not my father's. To my ear, my father's "God's will," sounded like got-swill. I ask, how can I, or anyone, take such an overworked notion seriously? Was there nothing on this earth that wasn't "Godswill?"

In those two years, he had gone from a sperm donor father who had left me to my own devices for the first eleven years of my life to an omnipresent broken record of god-swill-ings.

"I'll make it real easy for you. I am going to write that essay for you and then you will sign it," he said dictatorially. Mellifluous was nowhere to be found in his voice this time.

Still standing on the chair adjusting the Enola Gay as he left my room, my mind eagerly slipped away... *The plane broke through the edge of the hurricane into smooth air and leveled off. Since there was only a light crew manning the Enola Gay, I had been able to sneak aboard and hide in one of the side gun turrets. We must have been quite high up now, for I was getting very cold in that unheated part of the plane.*

I increased the angle of the suspended model to make it more dramatic, which better suited the swooping wanderings of my escapist mind. I really liked the drama of the angle but knew somewhere in the recesses of my brain that a bomber would never be in that position unless it was going to crash. But it looked so good from my bedroom door I left it that way.

"Are you working on it?" repeated my mother.

It took me a second to realize which "it" she meant: the questionnaire.

"Dad said he'd do it."

"When did he say that? He's not home yet."

"Huh?" Had I imagined him there in my room? It was one of those moments when I realized that I, as an only child, was spending too much time in my head. Or was it the What-If Story tyrant dragging me about? Or both! A What-If-Story about the Enola Gay, inside a What-If Story of my father, writing the essay? Wow! Fantastic!

"I mean, I need his help," I offered as a cover to my mother's question.

It was time to put my plan in motion. I climbed out of the gun turret, found a parachute, and put it on. No one seemed to be about. I took out my gun and moved toward the pilot's cabin. With my free hand, I jerked open the cabin door, rushed across the few feet that separated us and jabbed the gun into the pilot's left side just below his left shoulder blade, right in line with his heart. (According to my fifth-grade teacher the heart is located slightly left of center.)

"Change course, or I'll shoot." The co-pilot next to him swiveled to look at me.

"Turn around you," I said, taking command of the moment.

"IF YOU SHOOT ME, THE PLANE WILL CRASH," was the pilot's desperate response.

"No, it won't. The other guy will fly it. Shut up and take me to Montana." This was a "Sierra Madre" do-as-I-say film moment and I was Humphrey Bogart, the tough guy. (I loved Bogie).

"Montana...! Montana...? MONTANA?" said the pilot with mounting hysteria.

"We don't have enough fuel," the co-pilot responded coolly as he arrogantly tilted his nose at the cabin ceiling.

"What do you think I am, a stupid, twerpy kid? Montana or I'll shoot."

The two men looked at each other.

"And do it easy," I added.

The plane banked gently to the right till the compass pointed due west. I felt a euphoric surge of adrenaline. It felt great to turn the tables on grownups.

"Can I ask what's going on?" said the co-pilot.

"No."

"Why Montana? Not that it's any of my concern," said the pilot.

"No, it's not any of your concern."

"True. But I've got a right to know why I'm doing something that will ruin my life."

"You sound like you watch too many soap operas, like my mother."

"Well, maybe not ruin my life, but something unpleasant will happen."

"Do you really want to know?"

"Yes, I do," said the pilot. He turned to the co-pilot, "How about you?"

"Definitely," said the co-pilot in a more cooperative mood.

The excitement I felt at finding not one but two curious listeners, adults, I might add, was overwhelming. At last, someone wanted to hear my side of things. "My father," (I paused to snuffle for dramatic effect) "my father is sending me to a religious boarding school in New Market, Virginia." (I exhaled loudly). "He never asked me what I want to do. He acts as if he owns me. My life will never be the same. I want to go someplace far away so he can't find me. Someplace he'll never think to look."

The three of us looked at each other.

"What will you do there? I mean how will you stay alive?"

"In Montana? I'm gonna' live like a mountain man."

The two men made eye contact. They were trying to stifle smiles.

"Hey, wait a minute. What're you tryin' to do, sweet talk me?" I interjected between their smirks. It was a great line from a James Cagney movie, and I had always wanted to say it to a grownup. "You don't care at all, do you?"

"Of course, I do. My father wanted me to be a trapeze artist in the circus, like he was. Not a pilot. I ran away from home when I was fifteen."

"Wow. And you didn't want to do that? That sounds great to me."

"That's not the point. Kids shouldn't be bossed around by their parents like they own them."

"Yeah! Right!" I couldn't have agreed more. So, I said it again. "Right!"

I thought I heard a sound behind me and turned my head.

"Drop it, kid!"

There was a touch of cold steel against the base of my skull as an arm came around and grabbed my gun-hand. Before I could react, I was wrestled to the floor of the cabin and pinned down by two men.

I'm Not Here

"Who is this twerpy kid?

"I am not twerpy," I managed to garble. "I'm twelve and a half years old. I'm just short for my age."

The man who took away my gun was the navigator. "Where'd this kid come from?" he asked. "And look at this gun. It's a cap pistol."

The guy holding my head down on the floor with his foot was the bombardier. "You were hijacking this plane with a cap pistol?"

"It's Henry's, a kid I know. It's a beauty, ain't it? It's chrome-plated with a fake ivory handle grip. I thought it would be perfect for this caper."

"Yeah, it is, except it's still a cap pistol! Caper? You sound like you've been watchin' too many gangster movies, kid."

The plane began to bank back to the left and head south.

"Ahh, he's not so bad," said the pilot, "His father wants to send him away to a religious boarding school in Virginia without asking him if he likes the idea. He's desperate, and very upset. He has to leave all his friends and his model airplanes, especially the one of this very same plane that he just finished. And he has to leave his pet cat, Percival."

"Oh, that is terrible!" the navigator said. "You've got too much spunk for that, kid. And you know, if you think about it," he said to the pilot, "he really helped us by making us fly west. We missed the hurricane completely. "

I feigned a look of modesty and looked up sheepishly.

"Did you really name your cat Percival? Really?"

"Yeah. Something wrong with that?"

"Well, it's a sissy name," said the bombardier.

"Is not."

"Is so."

"Is not."

"Is so."

"Is not."

"Is so."

"Is n—"

"All right, enough you two," the pilot yelled.

"What are we gonna do with him?" asked the co-pilot. "It'll look strange if we show up with him when we land in Florida."

"Yeah, that's true. I been thinking about it and I think I've got an idea," said the pilot. "He wanted to parachute into the mountains of Montana to be a mountain man. Right, kid?"

"What a great idea," said the bombardier.

"We can't do that. There isn't enough fuel. Plus, the Army might think we're stealing the plane and send a fighter to shoot us down and well kid, we don't have any gunners or even bullets with us on this flight to defend ourselves."

Guessing where the pilot was going with this, the co-pilot offered, "How 'bout the mountains of West Virginia? Yeah!"

There was a general hubbub of "yeahs" among the men, which went on too long with far too much enthusiasm.

I started to object, "Hoow boot me? Don't I-eee augh, auw, ga, ga?" During their excited conversation, the bombardier had stomped down harder on my neck. He eased his foot back so they could understand me. "How 'bout me? Don't I get a say?" I repeated. "I don't know anything about West Virginia."

"NO," the four of them shouted immediately in unison.

All that sweet talk of theirs was just that—sweet talk. I was back to having no choice. Adults had taken over my What-if Story.

"Son, please accompany the bombardier back to the bomb bay. He'll help you get ready for your jump. We're nearly over the target now. Jump as soon as the bomb bay doors open, kid, or you might miss those tall, rugged West Virginia mountains."

His tone now seemed syrupy and phony, which reminded me of my father. Then he turned to the bombardier, and I heard him say under his breath, 'When I open the bomb bay doors, chuck the twerpy pain in the butt out."

He turned back to me, "We don't even know your name. What is it?" He was sweet-voiced again.

"Kilroy, to you. I heard you, you know."

I'm Not Here

"Cute. Very cute. Get Twerpy-pain-in-the-butt outta here," he snarled.

There's imagining the concept of parachuting out of an airplane when you're twelve and a half, as part of your brilliant What-If Story and then there is really imagining actually doing it when your twelve and a half years old.

Falling! Falling! Falling! I'm falling! I'm cold too! So cold. So very cold. Screaming! Screaming! I don't know what to do. I'm falling so fast I can't keep my mouth closed. I could choke on a bug!

Just pull the ripcord, dummy and stop wimping out, the other me told me.

So, I pulled the ripcord. The chute opened, slowing down my fall. I was drifting over a wide, pastoral valley. Small villages and farms were sprinkled throughout a bucolic landscape. Farm animals dotted verdant pastures. Young children with the family dog were rollicking about in their yard. There was also one field with at least 20,000 turkeys staring up at me. Life was good.

"Hey, wait a minute," I said to myself. "This doesn't look like the wild mountains of West Virginia. They threw me out in the wrong place."

No, they didn't, you dummy. You know they were going to just throw you out as soon as they could just to get rid of you, and that's what they did.

The ground was coming up fast. There were some buildings. I was crashing through tree limbs when everything suddenly stopped. I was scraped, cut, and bruised everywhere and swinging ever so gently back and forth about ten feet above the ground.

A door opened in a nearby building. A boy in his early teens, with a peach-fuzz face, walked over to the tree and looked up at me. He wore a frazzled straw hat, overalls with only one shoulder strap fastened, a red handkerchief in a back pocket, no shirt, a straw in his mouth, and he was barefoot and dirty. His face reminded me of David Von Endt, a boy from my eighth-grade church school class.

"How'd ye git thar' in this here tree?"

"I was trying to get to the mountains in West Virginia. Well, Montana originally."
"Oh. Well, ye did miss by a mite bit."
"Where am I?"
"Ya'all 'er in New Market, Virgin'ee."
"What?"
"Yup. At the Shenandoah Valley Academy."
"That's not possible," I protested.
"Why's that?"
"I worked so hard to not *be here."*
"But ya-all are here now."
"WHY?" I asked quite hysterically.
"It's Gotswill. Hallelujah!

At the age of twelve, when I was just beginning to have thoughts of my own, I found out that the grown-ups surrounding me didn't like it.

In 1952, my parents packed me in the back of their '49 Dodge four-door sedan with all my belongings and delivered me to Shenandoah Valley Academy, a Seventh Day Adventist boarding high school in New Market Virginia. Now Virginia in the early '50s was still the good-old-South and I, being from the bad-old-North, didn't quite fit in. Especially since I lived a mere 13 miles from "sinful" New York City. I talked funny, dressed funny, and my voice hadn't changed yet.

2

Disorientation

Have you ever been awakened at 6:00 AM by an alarm bell that was intended to be mounted on the front of a firehouse but was perversely installed, instead, on the hall wall immediately outside your bedroom door?

Some insidious sadistic church person back home, one of those wire-framed glasses, bun-on-the-back-of-her-head old lady types had said, about this school, in a soft saccharine tone, that a world of new, exciting, Godly surprises awaited me. Well, my first day started off—yes it did, way off—with a bang, which was my head meeting the bottom of the bunk bed above me. Missing from my first morning of exciting Godly surprises were the familiar dulcet tones of my mother's caressing voice at 7 AM, gently nudging me to wakefulness with a waiting hot breakfast.

My first thought this first morning, after my other real first thought, wondering where I was, was how to get out of there?

"Y'all better git your butt outta bed?"

Why did everything Rufus utter end in a question mark? And was the usage of butt bad language? It was bad language. 'Behind' was my northern word of choice.

My roommate was glaring at me from the doorway.

"Y'all got ten minutes to git downstairs?" He was a sophomore and I realized he knew the lay of the land. "Dressed?" he added with raised eyebrows and thin lips.

By now I was beginning to understand, as a fast, interpretive learner, the difference between Rufus' questions, which were few, and his attempt at declarative sentences. For a moment, I was having a difficult time remembering what it was that needed my presence downstairs. Then I leapt out of bed in near panic.

I avoided the bathroom across the hall, which was overwhelmed with eight boys for four sinks, and ambled—though it seemed an insanely demanding pace—toward the stairs, while trying to zip up my pants, button my shirt, comb my hair with my fingers, and put on my loafers—all while trying to stay upright when the eight boys from the bathroom rushed past me. I had forgotten socks.

I was on my way to morning worship in a subterranean chapel. The chapel was not only in the basement of the boy's dorm, it was airless, windowless, lit by too many fluorescent lights, and was painted an even worse bilious green than my room. My Pavlovian response as soon as the opening prayer began? I went to sleep.

"In my office right now," Mr. Feder proclaimed for everyone to hear.

I discovered morning worship was over.

"Oh good. I need to see you too," which elicited a strange look from him. I caught a sly smirk from David, my original intended roommate as he passed behind me. Did that smirk mean, oops you're in trouble or, not surprised? Or you're so pathetic?

David was the Golden boy from the Golden Family back in the Paterson church that we both attended.

At the top of the stairs I turned toward Dean Feder's office with the dean right behind me.

"You're not off to a good start are you Mr. Vice?" said Dean Feder.

Nor are you, I said to myself. *You broke your promise.*

"I'm not?" I responded naively.

"No, you're not... shoes unpolished, no socks, shirt buttoned crooked and you slept through *our* morning worship." He looked at me expectantly.

That "our" definitely did not include me.

I'm Not Here

Okay. Expect away. I've no intention of responding. I'd learned in the last few years that it never paid to volunteer anything with adults. Just look them in the eye innocently and wait.

"If you repeat that behavior Mr. Vice, you will be sent to detention…"

It seemed an impossibility for anyone to pronounce my name correctly. I don't know if it was the southern ear or if it signaled a judgment of character. I tried repeatedly to explain that Vis rhymes with kiss not vice. There were a few senior boys that got it, although with a less charming word for the rhyme.

Recalling the cramped daily schedule from my preliminary visit to tour the school with my parents just two weeks before, I couldn't imagine when they could squeeze in time for detention. Perhaps at four or five in the morning?

"…on Sunday afternoon," he continued. "Tomorrow you will be on time, properly dressed, and sitting in the front row. Do you understand?"

I nodded. He scrunched up his face, took a deep breath, and opened his mouth. Beating him to the punch I said, "Yes, sir"

As a dare against any possible audaciousness on my part, he asked "Any questions?"

It was the perfect opening. Deciding to take a chance I asked, "I thought that Charlie Sanderson from New Jersey was going to be my roommate, like you said?"

He exhaled loudly through his nose. "What has that to do with our talk?"

"I thought you were done. It's just that …" We looked at each other. Then I pushed ahead, "Could I have him as my roommate like you promised?"

"What about Rufus? Is there a problem?"

"He talks funny."

"Yes, and?"

"I can't understand half of what he says."

"You're the one that talks funny since most everyone is from the south. You'll get used to it. Stick with it a while longer, then we'll see."

"And he thinks I'm from evil New York City. Why would he think that?"

"Your clothes, your hair. You do know you look very different from everyone else." It was true I didn't like plaid shirts. "You should heed these words. Mr. Vice. It's Gotswill for you to fit into OUR happy family."

I found it interesting that 'God's will' was pronounced the same in the south as the north. Whenever it was used, I heard nothing else that followed it. Like a kind of ringing in my ears, it blotted out everything else. A disrespect I hoped God would not hold against me. I returned to my tried and true silence routine. I looked Feder in the eye with my own wide-open innocents.

"You may go now."

During the time I spent with him I managed to re-button my shirt and tuck it in my pants. As I left his office for the cafeteria, I re-ran my fingers through my tangled hair.

My hair was berserk. I broke combs regularly. I never knew from one morning to the next what it would do. Once straight and sandy blond as a toddler, it was now a rusty brown tangle of curls and waves and cowlicks, a perverse visitation that mitigated against an acceptable social appearance at that institution. As for my clothes, well, after all I was from a sizable town a good distance from this school, within thirteen miles of New York City.

As I entered the cafeteria a girl stationed at the door to assist freshman asked my name.

"Jerry... Vice," she finished. "Yes, you're at table 10. That's your table for the year."

"No, Vis. Rhymes with kiss." She looked confused.

"My name."

"Okay." She pointed me in the right direction.

Each table accommodated eight students, a boy, and a girl from each grade. The seniors sat head and foot at the table: boy at the head, girl at the foot. The rest of us sat opposite each other according to our year starting at the foot with freshmen.

"I suppose you have a good excuse for holding up our table?" said the senior boy.

I felt eroded by the acid glare of everyone's eyes. I timidly tried to explain to the tablecloth my run-in with Mr. Feder.

"No one is allowed to begin eating until everyone is present and seated and I give the word."

After a quick look at the food I figured I'd done everyone a favor.

"And I should add, properly dressed. Where are your socks?"

I smiled weakly. He was acting like an adult, so I didn't answer him.

Then we new students spent some time introducing ourselves to each other. Instead of eating, our table's host instructed us on the dining rules: always sit up straight, chew with your mouth shut, place your napkin in your lap, dress properly for meals, (this included a glance at me) finish everything on your plate, never rest arms on the table, one hand was to remain in ones lap if not being used, boys were to seat the girls, to name just some of them. I figured, hostilely, it would be essential for my mental health to skip meals unannounced.

"I would like you to say grace?" He was looking at me. It was the senior boy whose job it was to monitor behavior. This felt like a test.

The food still looked unappealing. "For that which we are about to eat we give thanks."

Job well done, I congratulated myself, though it was a lie. In no way was I thankful. And it probably wouldn't be the last lie of the day. But I'd try to keep my lies between me and God. Maybe he'd cut me some slack if I explained that this was a go-along-to-get-along survival situation.

"It's not 'eat.' The word is 'receive.' For that which we are about to receive..."

What could I say? It was the table rule that underclassmen were not to initiate conversation or respond unless directly addressed. This was not a conversation. "Nothing," is what I said. "Nothing." In this case, go-along-to-get-along had just bitten me in the butt. Or, rather, behind, because it's hard to talk while biting your tongue.

The senior girl's responsibility was to look after the needs of the table and supervise the underclassman as they served everyone. Other than that, she had little to add. It was absolutely the stiffest, most constricted meal I had ever eaten. It even exceeded lunch at David the Golden Boy's house back home. Maybe when I got to know everyone better it would change. With breakfast over, it was time for classes to start.

. . .

At lunch, I forgot to put my napkin in my lap. "Napkin Mr. Vice," said the commandant at the head of the table.

"Sorry. Please call me Jerry, okay?"

After lunch, all new students were to report back to their dormitory chapel to get their work assignments. It was a requirement that every student be gainfully employed.

There were fifteen boys present. Charlie's name was called, then Cassy, Ruppert, David, and so on. Everyone but me. Finally, Dean Feder called out my name, "Jerry Vice," as if the room were filled with a throng of waiting noisy boys. Everyone else had left for their appointed jobs.

"My name rhymes with kiss," I hissed under my breath.

"I'm not sure what to do with you." He looked up at me from his list.

I just sat silently looking at him for a moment from the rear of the room. "I thought I was supposed to work on the farm." I offered from my seat.

"Well why don't you report out there. See how it goes," his voice still booming.

The school ran a dairy farm to keep the boy's hands from idling in the Devil's playground. It also produced a cash crop of excellent dairy products, which they sold locally. After my less than enthusiastic send-off by the dean I made for the dairy in a contemplative slump. When was something going to make sense?

The farm manager, an old, crotchety, honest to goodness farmer in overalls was talking to six freshman boys standing along a small fenced-in area next to the milk house when I arrived. It turned out that not one of these mostly country boys had ever worked on a farm before, which evidently proved to be a great irritation to the farmer. Or so it seemed from his gruff tone. I arrived in the middle of an explanation about the different types of jobs to be done and who would do what, and when. The man looked sideways at me, "Late? Not a good start."

I had a good reason why I was late and was well into, "The dean kept me..." but he was already back on track. This was a no-win-go-along-and-get-screwed situation. That was strike three for my first morning. I joined the boys along the fence and hoped I'd never find out what it was like to work on a farm.

"We do our milkin' twice a day," the farmer continued, "three in the afternoon and again at three in the morning. Y'all 'er gonna' rotate through those times plus do other chores.

Was he serious? Three in the morning? The Devil's playground was definitely looking good to me.

David was one of the boys. "You gonna' do that David?" I asked later.

He shrugged, "Sure." *Like-why-wouldn't-I* implied.

The farmer went down the line handing out jobs and schedules and pairing the boys up with older boys to learn what to do. Then he turned to me, walked right up in front of me and just stood there looming over me, his chin against his chest. It was meant to intimidate, and it did until he spoke. He took a deep breath and said, "What am I supposed to do with you?" his head bobbing up and down against his wedged chin.

Trying not to snicker I wondered if that was a question he expected me to answer. All the adults in my life back home had thus far had no lack of ideas for what to do with me. That's how I got to be at this school, standing there talking to this here farmer. I had no helpful suggestions, so I just stood there staring up at him.

He finally moved slightly away. "How old are you?"

"Twelve. And a half," I added.

"Twelve! You look like y'all 'er eight. How tall are ya?"

"Four foot ten."

"Four ten, four ten. Too short for drivin' equipment or anythin.' How much you weigh?"

"Ninety pounds, I think."

"Okay, all right. Y'all got sent out here to me. I guess I need to find somethin' for y'all to do. Follow me." We walked over to one of several silos. "Climb up there and git inside. Y'all are gonna 'tramp silo.'"

"What's that?"

"We're fillin' the silo with chopped cow corn. All y'all got to do is walk round inside to pack the corn shocks down."

There were removable hatches up the side of the silo. About a third of the way up one was open. I climbed up the ladder and looked in. About ten feet below was the silage level.

"Don't look at it. Get y'all's butt in there."

"How'll I get out?"

"When it fills up y'all will git out. Go on now, Git."

The hatch was so small I couldn't figure out how to get in feet first so yielding to yelling from the ground, I dove in headfirst instead. I sank in nearly up to my waist, pulled myself up, spitting out chopped corn shocks. Then the silage began to rain down on me from the top of the silo. It was like the blizzard of '47. I couldn't see a thing. I walked round and round trying not to breathe through my mouth, though I needed to. I kept my hands cupped over my eyes to keep the junk out of them. I thought of my Grandmother when she was my age, taken out of school by her father to start work in the weaving mills in Paterson. "She's had enough education for a girl," he told the teacher when he stormed into the classroom and pulled Ada up out of her desk. I hadn't moved up much in the world.

Maybe two hours later the farmer stuck his head in. I was nearly up to the open hatch. "You're useless. I've got nothin' for you to do out here. Y'all 'er too little. Now I got to git four useful boys to come in here, waste their time re-tramping this here silo. Plus, you ain't got the sense of a rooster, divin' in headfirst. Don't bother comin' back no more."

"Thank you," I said.

The startled farmer's jaw dropped. And I went skipping off the quarter-mile back to the dorm chanting "Thankque, thankque, thankque." To my surprise that made two adults in one day that didn't know what to do with me. I was making real progress.

I arrived back at the dorm looking like the scarecrow from The Wizard of Oz. "Git outta here, I just swept the floor," said a large boy leaning on a broom in the entryway. "When you shake off all that trash, I'll let you in." The boy was very big and very, very mean-looking. I backed out onto the porch. "Go on. Y'all er not comin' in here till I say so. Take 'em off and shake 'em out."

So, I took off my shirt and pants to shake them off, which left me standing on the front porch in view of the girl's dorm and the world in my underwear. In an attempt to distract myself from being mortified, my mind said if I were only wearing a bathing suit, I'd not have a care in the world. I wanted the broom-boy's blood. So, believing I'd been humiliated long enough, I spun around to face my torturer. He was gone and the Boy's Dean was standing in the doorway.

"Git your butt in here. What is wrong with you? This makes the third time today I have had to speak to you. And it's only your first day here."

I thought it was only twice, but figured I'd better not correct him. Besides, I was feeling so corn-shock itchy it was all I could do to look like I cared about what he was saying for more than fifteen seconds. There might have been more on his mind. He looked like a man with an ample supply of complaints, so I darted by him and the dorm office door where I saw the brute with the broom and another boy at a desk laughing. Our eyes met momentarily. And there were still five hours left in the day 'til lights out. What else could go berserk?

I made it up the stairs without further difficulty, ran down the hall, and burst through my door to find Rufus on his knees next to my bed with his hands clasped against the edge and his drooling face burrowed into my chenille bedspread.

"What are you doing there?"

"Prayin'."

"At four in the afternoon?" I silently threw up my arms, shook my head, and turned away to strip off the rest of my clothes. I draped a towel across my shoulders, grabbed a bar of soap, and ran across the hall where I nearly collided with two man-size boys drying off after a shower. At the age of twelve I had only seen adult males from the waist up. What existed below was as unknown to me as the opposite sex. I mean of course, I knew what boys looked like. And had seen plenty of naked boys. I had gone to the Paterson "Y" summer program when I was eight and nine. We all swam in the buff. No big deal. As I stood there staring at them, I realized I didn't want these two to see me nude. They had hair everywhere. I had absolutely none anywhere below my eyelashes.

"Hey, what are y'all lookin' at?" said the boy with red hair.

"Look at him. He looks like a little girl."

I was facing them with my hands now covering my crotch.

"What y'all hidin' there? Let us have a peak," said the red-haired boy.

I'm Not Here

I tried to jump into a shower stall. In addition to my itching, I was also mortally embarrassed again, and only a few minutes away from the last time.

"No. No. Y'all can't move if a Senior is talkin' to you. Now let's see. You saw us. Now it's our turn. Show us yours." They moved up next to me and pulled my hands away.

"What do you think, Delmer, is it a boy or a little girl?"

"Well, you know I'm not sure. Maybe it could be a girl. Ain't no titties yet though. Wait, what is that little thing 'tween your legs?" Delmer asked me. "Is it real? Looks like a piece of your baby sister's pinky."

They both doubled over laughing. I got loose, jumped into the shower, slammed the door shut and turned on the water with my towel still draped across my shoulders. I figured I still had about four hours and thirty minutes left 'til lights-out.

In retrospect, I should have joined Rufus, drooling into my chenille bedspread. But then I wouldn't have known what I should be thankful for.

In looking back, I can see that my northern self and those southern others were equally prejudiced. But, you couldn't have told me that at the time. I protest even now in self-defense because I was so outnumbered. That should count for something. (It never does).

Words to live by: "If thy right eye offend thee, pluck it out, and cast it from thee." In my case, it should have been my lack of hair.

At every possible opportunity, I was informed that day that the woes that beset me were of my own doing. Some were.

A Teenage Lament:

Oh Damn! Must I?
Always.
I'll give it a try someday.
No. Right now.

3

THINKS AGAIN

"Ayah. My futhah pahked his cah ne-ah the watah so's he could dump the tiahs in the habah. But 'e got caught."

That was Bart's answer to my question: "What did your father do that got him in trouble? Would you tell me?" In translation, this is what he said. "Yes. My father parked his car near the water so he could dump the tires in the harbor. But he got caught."

We were a good way into the school year when Barton appeared. The boy's dean had promised me Charlie Sanderson from New Jersey, a fellow Yankee, for my roommate. Instead, I got Rufus, a preacher's son from the deep south that spoke an impenetrable language. I was told it was I that spoke the impenetrable language and that I should forget about a different roommate. Then, sometime in October, Rufus asked Dean Feder if he could have a different roommate. It seemed I confused him. I talked funny, among other things. That's when Barton Barber from Bar Harbor, Maine, moved in with me. We were a perfect match, according to Dean Feder, since we were both from the North, and I should have no trouble understanding him.

The conversation that began this tire story started with, "Why are you starting the school year so late, Bart?

Basically, he told me his mother was trying to keep him safe. His parents were in the midst of a custody battle over him. Stuff came to a standstill when his father got arrested for dumping the tires. He was in jail. So, his mother seized the moment and got Barton out of town.

I'm Not Here

"Wow! Are your parents Adventists?" I couldn't put this together. This wasn't typical behavior of any Adventist family I knew. "Is your father an Adventist? No, he couldn't be. Just your mother?"

No. She was just hiding him. I thought I might mention my attempted hijacking story to get to Montana to avoid being trapped here. Sort of like: we're in this together, Bart, to make him more willing to tell me what was going on. It didn't make sense that someone would be arrested just for dumping tires in a harbor. But as I dwelled upon the idea, I realized this was way beyond anything going on in my life. I was impressed. Bart was very nonchalant about it all, like—it's just another day. So, I dropped it.

Heading to more familiar ground, I asked, "What do you think about this place?"

"It seems really weird. All we do is go to church every day. We don't even go to any church back in Bar Harbor."

Thank God, an ally. "So, how did she pick this place?"

"Her sister, my aunt. She's Adventist. She set the whole thing up. Pretty clever, huh?"

"And your father? What does he think of it?"

"He doesn't know, and he'll never find me either. He'll kill 'er when he gets out."

After several hours wading through his accent, and he through mine, that was the gist of it. It didn't matter because immediately I like Bart.

But how could I have possibly gotten two roommates in a row within the first two months that didn't speak English? I realized during one daydreaming moment, the Eastern United States and Switzerland had one thing in common: they both had three official languages.

I also really, really liked Bart because he wasn't inclined to fall onto his knees multiple times a day and drool all over my bedspread. And, we liked the same thing: getting as far away from the school as often as possible. We began to do everything together. One day we went into town. We were permitted one trip to the village a month. My trip usually included a stop at the barbershop. Bart wasn't interested, so we parted company for a while.

The shop appeared to be as typical as any barbershop I'd ever been to, marked by its rotating striped barber's pole out front. But that was where the similarity ended. Inside the walls, above the large shop mirror, was an extraordinary collection of stuffed dead animals: deer heads with large antler racks, running rabbits on a shelf, a fox or two, several hawks, and an owl. I'd never seen a stuffed dead animal. Only had an abstract city boy's understanding of such. The real thing was amazing, exotic. My barbershop at home had black and white pictures of local ball teams in that same place of honor, which did nothing for anyone except, more than likely, the fathers of the boys in the pictures.

This shop differed in another way. All the customers got the same haircut –no sideburns, neck shaved in the back, even with the top of their ears as if a bowl had been placed on their heads. That was the treatment I received the first time.

This was my third time, and I was prepared to break with local tradition, though I entered the shop with great trepidation, ready to do battle if need be, to get a hairstyle that I wanted, a flat top, crew cut. I had no faith in this aged man's willingness to understand something so different, let alone my northern pushiness. I was an in-the-know northern kid, and I intended to let anyone in the barbershop and back at the school know it. I had come prepared with a picture.

It was a busy day with three men waiting and one in the chair. Which suited me just fine. Not because I was nervous about my intentions, but because of the magazines—magazines forbidden at the school. This barbershop, like barbershops everywhere on the planet, had an assortment of men's magazines available for waiting customers. It was a feast to have a stack of magazines to look through. The only periodicals available in our library were church publications. The barbershop had everything from the semi-risqué Esquire to the equally forbidden-at-school, but my favorite, Argosy magazine, filled with tales of adventures. This issue included an article on the Second World War bombing of Dresden. It was a sampler feast to have such a stack of magazines to peruse. And peruse I did like an island castaway eating his first real meal in months. But that piece on Dresden was very disturbing. It somehow caught me off guard. The article claimed we, America and our allies, bombed the city non-stop, day and night, for a month. The city of Dresden, considered one of the most beautiful in Europe, had no military or manufacturing value. The duration of the attack caused a firestorm that engulfed the entire city, killing over one hundred thousand civilians. The fire's need for oxygen was so great it created winds in excess of eight hundred miles per hour at its base, sucking burnable materials and living beings into the fire from great distances.

When it was my turn, I brought the magazine with me to the barber's chair.

"Can I please finish this story about Dresden while you cut my hair?" I asked. I knew that was not likely and too assertive, but there was something so startling, even more troubling, about this Dresden information, killing one hundred thousand people (before Hiroshima) with blockbuster bombs.

"'Fraid not."

Not forcing the issue, I took out the picture of the haircut I wanted. "Do you think you could do this?"

He looked at the picture without comment for some time.

"Y'all 'll look like a Marine. That what you want?"

There was something about the man that I liked. He was in his sixties, ruddy-faced and nearly bald. He was always friendly and patient with my Yankee speech.

"No. I want the sides long."

"Long? How long?"

"Normal long, like you always do."

I climbed up in the chair with a vague apprehension that a looming grooming disaster was about to occur. But since I was from New York, well almost, then I darn well should look the part. I could have waited a few weeks and got my hair cut at Hollywood Joe's barbershop during Thanksgiving break back home, but what good is it to be twelve years, ten months old if you can't be impulsive from time to time.

"Y'all readin' that piece on Dresden? Fantastic huh? Guess we showed them Nazis."

The top inch of my head looked like the flat-top crew cut I wanted, from there down to my ears, long on the sides. Okay. But from my ears down, I was shaved clean to my shiny pink skin in the barber's usual way. I wanted to hide. The barber had wanted to know if it was what I wanted. I suppose I could have had him finish the Marine haircut by making the sides short too, but like a person fleeing a burning building, I wanted to get out of there as fast as possible. "Yeah' it looks okay," I said. "Bye."

"Oh. Y'all wanna hang on to the magazine to finish the Dresden thing? It's fine with me. Bring it back when y'all 're done."

I realized I was on my way out the door with the rolled-up magazine in my hand. I thanked him. When I got back outside, I tucked it into the top of my pants and pulled my shirt down to hide it so that I could smuggle it back into the dormitory.

Why had that article affected me so? And it was the article, more than the ridiculous haircut, that froze the place and events in my memory.

I can picture that barbershop that day, as clearly as my own childhood bedroom. I was seated next to the small magazine table, barely able to contain its unstable ear-worn stack. All the other chrome leatherette chairs against the wall were filled with waiting customers. The glaring bright whiteness of the room forced me to shield my eyes with my left hand. And then there was the vague scent of talcum powder, too sweet, in the narrow room and the background hum of southern banter about shooting rabbits while I read on about Dresden.

I'm Not Here

• • •

Bart found me on the street outside the barbershop. "Holy hell, what happened to you?"

"That bad?"

"You look like you escaped from a crazy house. I don't want to be near you when we get back to school."

I ignored him and asked, "You hungry? There's a restaurant across the street that sells pizza. You ever had it?" In 1952 pizza was unheard of in the Shenandoah Valley of Virginia.

"No, what's that?"

"It's Italian. It's a big flat pie covered with tomato sauce an' cheese." I had been eating them back home in Paterson for the last few years, and I missed them.

Paterson was one of the few cities to have pizza just after the Second World War. I hadn't seen any evidence of Pizza Parlors since coming south. So, I was quite surprised on my last trip to the village to find there was a place that had pizza on their menu, along with grits n' gravy and southern fried chicken. I was suspicious that they might not really know how to make it, but anything would be a step up from the uninspired, even demoralizing food at school, where everything was overcooked, unseasoned, and subject to the church founder's restricted foods list. Not even salt was permitted in the dining hall. There was butter on the table, but that was only intended for the bread. I used it on my food, along with salt and pepper that I began smuggling to every meal.

Despite initial resistance, everyone at my table began to use my salt and pepper. It made me feel gleefully perverse: a missionary con-man in the righteous land of culinary deprivation.

• • •

It was too early for supper, so the restaurant was empty, sparing me unwanted attention. We ordered our pie. They only made a tomato pie, no toppings. The waitress brought out a knife, a fork and a spoon, and a bowl of hot liquid. I wasn't sure what the silverware was for since you eat pizza by picking it up.

"What's the bowl for?" Bart was looking for insider information on the way to eat pizza.

"I don't know."

"You're the one that's had pizza."

"I don't know. Maybe it's soup—comes with the pizza."

"You ever get soup with pizza back home?"

"Nah. But this is the south. They do things we don't know about."

So we tasted it.

"Not much flavor." Bart was making slurping sounds while concentrating and staring at a spot on my forehead like he was a food critic.

We added salt and pepper.

"That's not much better," I said.

Bart kept at it: adding salt, slurping away. I gave up halfway through. When the waitress came out with the pizza, she looked at Bart's bowl and said, "Oh, you need more water for your finger bowl."

The pie was in a glass pie plate covered with florescent red sauce and melted cubes of some sort of equally bright yellow cheese. Whatever it was, it wasn't pizza, but it was tasty.

While we sat there eating our southern version of a northern version of Italy's pizza, I began to tell Bart about the article in Argosy.

"I can't get it out of my mind."

"Let me see it. I don't understand. Why's it got you so upset?"

It was still tucked under my clothes. I stood up to get it out and walked around the table to show him the article.

"Look at these pictures. They're unbelievable. They destroyed Dresden the way they did Hiroshima. Only they didn't have the atom bomb to do it."

"Yeah. You said it took them a month?"

"I think so. Maybe longer. Can you imagine being in that city waiting for the air raid to be over? Only it never is."

• • •

The meals at the school dining room were repeated on a regular schedule. As time went on, I added mustard, ketchup, or Worcestershire sauce for evening meals, whatever seemed right for that day, and raspberry preserve, my favorite, for breakfast and sundry other comestibles that absolutely no one at my table voiced any objections to. They even worked hard at hiding things as they were passed around the table.

Like clockwork, once a month on the same day in the same week, the school kitchen went out on a limb to make a meal more intensely flavored than over-cooked peas, something called Dago Stew. Amazing. Where I came from, Dago was an insulting name for Italians. And as for the stew, it was no more Italian than hot dogs and sour kraut. It consisted of boiled potatoes, carrots, and onions drowned in a thick red tomato paste straight out of a number 10 tin can. For this, I brought garlic salt to the table. It didn't help.

• • •

Bart was right. I was tormented about my haircut for days and days. I knew that keeping a low profile was best. But then there are times when being an in-your-face-contrarian is irresistible. My aim was to be the coolest, in-the-know guy on campus since the opposite, local look, was beyond my ability. I missed that target which everyone was delighted to point out. Plus, both Dean Feder and the school minister called me out on my appearance. Not only was I being belligerent (their word), I was aping degenerate, worldly trifles. Foppish was another word Pastor Milner used. I had to look that one up. Well, it was true to some extent. I did have an insatiable desire for whatever was new, be it hairstyles or clothing. And it surely didn't include the latest look in plaid shirts, white socks, chino pants, or buzz haircuts.

Perversely, the words from Popeye the sailor man, kept running through my head during my dressing down by our minister, "It's not easy being me." Now I was feeling sorry for myself on top of feeling stupid.

4

Goin' Home, Goin' Home, Lord I'm Goin' Home

My haircut created a lot more trouble than I ever could have imagined. In addition to Pastor Milner, the boy's dean, my roommate, and snickers behind my back, the Senior boys now had reason to notice me again. One afternoon, I decided to shower in the afternoon when no one would be around. The senior boys found me, pulled me from the shower, and held me upside down, stark naked from the third-floor window by my heels, just for their amusement and for all the world to see, including the girls hanging laundry on the clotheslines below. From then on, I began receiving notes in my laundered underwear about my cuteness from the girls who worked in the laundry.

So, I sat down in desperation one afternoon after work to make a list of everything that was going wrong. I'm not sure what purpose I thought it might serve, but I was feeling guilty about feeling sorry for myself and wanted to make sure I was on the right track.

Things That Aren't Good:
1. Still getting notes in my underwear. Don't want to send laundry there.
2. Senior boys back on my ass because of haircut. Afraid to take showers again.
3. Some of the senior laundry girls want to find me a girlfriend as cute as me. Think I should get another haircut.

4. Boy's dean after me to dress right and get my haircut.

5. Rev. Milner demands I attend his Baptismal Class to rid me of my vain ways and get my hair cut.

6. Gotten out of bed at ten PM, not allowed to find a bath robe, then taken to Dean Feder's office in my underwear where the creepy dean looked me up and down the whole time.

7. My Uncle Phil's weird urgent phone call asking me to come home so he could tell me his plan for the rest of my life.

8. After dumping me off at the school two months ago, I still haven't heard anything from my parents.

9. Don't have any money to get home for Thanksgiving.

And just to make sure I was being fair, I did a "good" list.

Things That Are Good:
1. My old roommate Rufus moved out.
2. My new roommate isn't a religious loony.
3. Going on walks. Exploring caves.
4. Schoolwork is real easy.
5. Don't have any money to get home for Thanksgiving.

So, I was on the right track! The only good things had little to do with the school, except maybe schoolwork. But that was a good thing. Really good.

Just before the Thanksgiving break, I needed to add number ten to the Things that aren't good list. I was starting to smell a bit ripe because of the laundry/shower problem, and others were starting to notice. Since being hung out the window, I was afraid to take showers and too embarrassed to send my clothes to the laundry.

Finally, a letter from home arrived with money and instructions for the trip. My mother had figured out the timetable for trip connections. I had to get to New Market early, 6 AM, to get the bus to D.C. The only way at that hour was to walk to the village. I caught the bus to D.C., took a taxi to Union Station, got the train to Newark, then a bus to Paterson, didn't have any money for the local bus to my house, so I walked the last mile home where my mother greeted me with a tear-soaked hanky and a veggie-burger sandwich (Adventists are vegetarians) and, most gratefully, a hot cup of caffeine-laden Salada Tea.

The next week was the most bizarre week of my life. For the very first time, my mother's parents came to have Thanksgiving dinner with us. My Grandparents, I had learned through osmosis, had never liked my father. And now they hated him for coercing my mother into leaving the Baptist Church for the "lunacy of Adventism." I remember they arrived quite late. My mother was still fussing over the table setting, running back and forth from the kitchen stove to the dining room where she kept nudging the silverware, purchased on time, so that it was flush with the bottom of the blue-edged dinner plates we'd never used before.

Only my grandmother spoke the whole time, and then, only to my mother. We all sat down without a sound except my father, who was still walking around in the backyard. My grandfather, never one to waste words, asked me a few terse questions. Not about school or the south, but what it was like to be stuck living with all those Adventists and did I remember my promise to never become one? This all transpired before my father sat down. From then on, the only sounds came from the deafening clank of silverware irritating the dinner plates.

They left before the dessert my mother made specially for my grandfather. My mother had gone out to the kitchen to get it. When she returned, her parents were standing next to their chairs, putting on their coats. My grandmother looked at my mother where she had stopped, dessert in hand, a few feet from the table and said, "The Timmerman's asked us for Thanksgiving dinner at four," and they turned and left.

The next day I went upstairs to see my Uncle Phil in his apartment. I had to wait until my Aunt Fay went to work. I had heard her screaming at him through the floor. When I got there, he didn't remember that he had called me at school. The call seemed so urgent, I couldn't imagine him not remembering. I loved him so much and was hurt he didn't remember. But then, he never remembered much of anything beyond a few minutes if he had lost interest in it. That's why he and my Aunt were arguing again, I was sure. She was one of those things he had lost interest in. My mother and I pretended we never heard them arguing whenever my Aunt came downstairs to offer an apology, which I was sure she did to gain my mother's sympathetic ear.

The moment I walked through my Uncle's living room door, I knew what the fight was about. He had gotten a high-fidelity record player and the packing, which was shredded wood fibers at that time, was scattered all over my Aunt's carefully decorated room.

When I reminded him about the call, he got an excited glint in his eye and suggested we go out for breakfast. I supposed for the chance to get away from the scene of the living room debacle and the withering echo of his wife's voice. We went to Bickford's across the street from the Erie train station, his favorite place to hide from his spouse. The counterman knew him and automatically brought two coffees to our table. Phil filled his cup until it was overflowing, adding about six heaping spoons of sugar, then ordered corned beef hash and two over easy's for both of us. The food arrived just as he started to explain the reason for the call. I sat quietly waiting for his ritual of burying his food in salt, pepper, and ketchup, after which he resumed his abandoned sentence, "...so if you learn Russian..." at which point he glanced around the empty room and asked me to get him more ketchup from a neighboring table. He then devoted himself exclusively to eating while I floated along in a state of suspended apprehension. He finished quickly, looked up, and, thinking I was not hungry, reached for my untouched plate and proceeded to eat my breakfast too. Only then did he pick up the thread of conversation about his plan for my entire life, which consisted of sending me to Russia at his expense to study art so I would be able to make beautiful posters for the Marxist Revolution about sharing the world's wealth equally. He assured me that the revolution was on the brink of sweeping the planet as he finished my corned beef hash and eggs. While he waited for my response, which was quite catatonic, he asked if I was still hungry.

What could I say? I said, "No."

I was simultaneously disappointed and flattered at his proposal. He was the only adult who had ever talked to me as if I were an intelligent being. The only adult that helped me to understand the world around me. He taught me to play chess. He told me I should become an artist. He taught me it's what you find between the lines in the newspapers that is the most revealing, and that a good education teaches you how to use your mind. And now, ironically, he was telling me what to do! Bribing me! Just like all the other adults—Milner, my father, everyone, even the church—with something I didn't want. That was crazy.

Later that afternoon, I got a buzz hair cut at the local barbershop. My parents agreed with everyone else that a flat-top with long sides had to go. That evening I had to keep an appointment—*an appointment!*—with my father to discuss my future. This is the gist of what transpired. In the eyes of the Adventist church, I would be at the age of "accountability" on my 13th birthday. Meaning from then on, anything I did that was wrong would be a sin. I guessed that meant that my days of a free ride in the eyes of God were about to come to an end. Therefore, I should be baptized to avoid an accountability gap. My father was planning to sign me up for baptismal classes during Christmas vacation at the Paterson church with all those fellow church kids coming of age. Up until that point, I hadn't been required to say anything. In this regard, my Uncle's message and my father's seemed very much alike. He made the mistake of asking, "Okay?"

It was a rhetorical question. I knew that. But the first and only words out of my mouth were, "I hate school down there." I might only be twelve, but I was very tired of done deals.

I watched him bristle. My mother turned away and began to saturate her second hanky of the weekend. I got up and walked out of the room. Two days later, I got on my three-speed English Racer bike and, without a word to anyone, peddled thirteen miles to the George Washington Bridge and evil, evil New York City where I rode around for an hour out of spite and revenge, feeling the freest I'd felt since the summer before boarding school.

The next morning, I was looking out the train window at the compressed urban tangle that was north Jersey. There seemed to be a peculiar, dense, airless pressure to the landscape as if the volume of all the buildings, and people, and traffic, and gray air were weighing down upon it. It made me feel asthmatic and shriveled, as the maze of unrelated things and movement, much like my week at home, passed indifferently by the window of the train, leading me nowhere. Maybe the train would wreck. That would be nice. Or maybe it would get lost, and I'd get off in some other country. But no. It was Washington, ahead of schedule according to the conductor. He made a tour of the train, stopping in each car to announce, like a proud first-time father, that our engineer was running the train at one hundred eight miles an hour, and we'd be arriving in D.C. twenty minutes early.

Okay, a train wreck it is then.

Instead, I caught the bus out of D.C. into the rural blankness of Virginia that no longer held my interest. It, too, felt as dense and airless as the urban north. It amused me to think of the emptiness of Virginia weighing the same as north Jersey. Then I found myself on the street in New Market, watching the bus escape south down route eleven without me. And I realized how intensely things, both innocuous and dreaded, had troubled me deeply. Exhausted, I turned to begin the walk from the village to the school.

I'm Not Here

I remember standing at the corner watching the bus disappear down the road in one direction, then looking down the other direction that led to the school, feeling feelings I never knew existed with not the slightest inclination to move, longing for the bravado I'd need, even a false rehearsed version, that would mean I hadn't given in.

The soft touch of a kind human hand would have felt so good.

5

There's No Place Like Home for the Holidays

It had only been a few weeks since my Thanksgiving visit home, but an enormous new development had occurred. My mother could no longer understand large chunks of what I was saying. Unbeknownst to me, I had acquired a southern lilt. Endless repetitions and alternative explanations were now needed for language that seemed totally understandable to me. For instance, she wanted to know how I was feeling after my long trip home for Christmas.

"A'm tar'd."

I could tell from her face that she was working her way through the syntax and contractions, searching for a possible meaning. Not that it was an impossible task, just an unfamiliar one. She was going through what I had been going through for three months. It was a funny awareness. Made me realize I needed to slow my speech. All was resolved in a few days as I rediscovered how to speak North Jersey.

• • •

I woke late the Sunday morning before Christmas. A familiar mix of voices reached me from the kitchen. My father and Uncle Phil were sitting at our worn Formica table discussing the election of President Eisenhower that past November.

"He's not a Democrat," said my father, "but he's a good man. What's your problem with him?"

"He'll be coming after people like me."

"Oh. Because you're a commie?"

There was a definite, familiar edge to the air as I eased into the room.

My father turned and glared at me. "We need to talk."

I avoided eye contact and sat down on the other side of the table.

"Yes," responded my uncle, "Because I'm a communist. Maybe he is a good man, but the Republicans control both houses. And there's no counterbalance of a Democrat in the White House. They'll go after everything Roosevelt did to help people. You just wait. There's going to be a paranoid Republican witch hunt against those of us that want a more equitable world. You know, one where they might have to share it with the rest of us."

"Would you like some breakfast, Jerry?" My mother was at the stove, humming tunelessly to herself as she stirred up some eggs in our cast iron pan.

"Yes, Mom. Thanks." I poured myself a cuppa coffee. God how I missed these heated Sunday morning political discussions. Both my uncle and father started on their second cups of coffee while my uncle made sandwiches filled with butter and ketchup, made with Verp's Bakery hard rolls. These circular talks always ended with my father pretending to be right of center and my uncle reminding him of the egalitarian New Testament Beatitudes and one of his knife-edged ironic thoughts: "you know, Jesus was the first communist." Uncle Phil was a pro at getting in the final shot. After he went back upstairs, my father turned to me and said, "I've signed you up for Baptismal Class with Pastor Quigley. It starts tomorrow."

"I've already—"

"You've already what?" my father asked, "Taken those lessons? I talked to Pastor Milner at your school two days ago to see how you were doing. You never took them."

I never would have believed it possible to have a lump in my throat, a sinking feeling in my stomach, and weak knees all at once, but... I had to accept that the battle was lost.

The class met Monday, Wednesday, and Friday, for the next two weeks, with the actual Baptism scheduled for the following Sabbath, on the third of January.

• • •

Methodist, Baptist, Dutch Reform, Adventist: it didn't matter what church we were going to. We celebrated Christmas Eve the same way. We decorated the tree, had our usual large dinner just before midnight, opened presents afterwards. Uncle Phil and Aunt Fay had come down from their apartment on the second floor to join us with their two daughters, Connie and Phyllis. The grownups started telling cute stories about us kids when we were little. Mine was about how my parents tricked me into believing in Santa Claus until I was ten. My father had gotten a black eye in some stupid scuffle at the bar next store. But he and my mother told me he got it from Santa's bag as he swung it up onto his shoulder as Santa was leaving the house. Would there ever come a time when I was too old to not be a victim of my own supposed cuteness?

Then Uncle Phil began a story about his two daughters when they lived over Vigliano's Bar down the street. There was no connection with Christmas since it happened in the summer. At the time, Connie was eight and Phyllis seven. It seems Connie had been a sleepwalker, to such an extent that Phil often had to leave his bed in the middle of the night to look for his daughter while she wandered down the back stairs into the street. Since his daughters slept together in the same bed, he decided to remedy the situation by tying Connie's ankle to Phyllis'. Thus, if Connie tried to get out of bed, she would wake her sister. It was a warm, still night. The neighborhood was quiet 'til Phil and Fay heard yelling outside their kitchen porch door. When they went to find the source of the noise, they discovered that sleepwalking Connie had dragged her sleeping sister out of bed, through the kitchen, and halfway down the porch stairs where Phyllis had finally woken up.

"Did I mention they were both naked? It was so hot." he added.

He finished the story to a silent room. His daughters, now eighteen and seventeen, were not amused. No one knew where to look. Several moments passed, then Uncle Phil turned to me and said, "Jerry. I forgot to give you your Christmas present. Here's $20.00 to buy a recorded set of Russian lessons so you can study art in Russia when you finish high school."

My father jumped to his feet, "What did you say?"

Fay jumped to her feet and said, "I've had enough of this ____Phil. I'm going to bed."

I stood, reached across the table, and took the money. I didn't mention that we were not allowed to have a record player at Shenandoah.

"Thanks Uncle Phil," was all I said. I thought, maybe I shouldn't take the money. It was under false pretenses but the expanse of numbing time I knew it would have taken to explain something, plus the fact that he wouldn't understand, and that it would hurt his feelings too...

Phil's two daughters didn't jump up at all. They didn't move or make a sound. They sat there in a catatonic state.

My mother asked if anyone wanted any more mulled cider.

The next day I asked her if that story of Phil's was true.

"True? I've heard it before," was her oblique answer.

"Why did Aunt Fay get so angry? And Connie and Phillis look that way? If it was true?"

"Most people think you have a mental problem if you're a sleepwalker. That maybe there's something wrong with your family. That you're trying to get away from something bad."

"So, is it true then?"

"Yes. But every time I've heard it, it changes. This time they were naked, and Phyllis couldn't wake up. And then there was a part he left out. Several times the police supposedly found Connie and had to bring her home."

"Is that true too?"

My mother shrugged.

. . .

I attended every Baptismal class for two weeks. Studied all the lessons, answered all the questions, and passed the program successfully. David was also in the class, as well as four other church kids, all of us thirteen. Pastor Quigley took each of us, individually, into his office to ask the most important question of our young lives: are you willing to be baptized?

"You've completed the classwork. I think you're ready to be baptized, Jerry. Do you?"

This was the first adult I had encountered who had ever asked me my opinion.

Unable to look at him directly, I said "No."

"No? That's surprising. Why not? Do you understand the significance of this decision? You did well in the classes."

Here it comes. The Lecture.

"Do you accept that Christ is your personal savior? That he will be coming again to gather the righteous home to heaven? Those baptized in his name? If you're not baptized you will not be able to go there."

This was not the first time I'd heard this, and it was not the first time I'd wondered what would happen to all the people on earth that might not know about this, that were Hindu or something or born and died long, long ago?

I really didn't know this man. He was quiet, said all the things ministers always said. Looked the part. It made me uncertain about my answer. Or, not so much my answer as his response. I looked up and hesitated.

I'm Not Here

His office was a small room to the left of the sanctuary beyond the nave. Its window looked out on the church schoolyard where I played in as an eighth-grader. He asked why I kept looking out the window. I knew he knew it was something other than a way to delay my answer. The silence had gone on too long. I was remembering the day I was at the fence by the sidewalk to get a ball David had just thrown to me. A bunch of my friends that I grew up with were passing by on the sidewalk five feet away, on their way to P.S. 12, my school too, until eighth-grade. They wouldn't say hello. After all, my parents had joined that weird church.

I said, "I just don't want to," then I turned to look him in the face.

Pastor Quigley looked at me for a few seconds then said, "You've put in a good effort. I believe you understand the church's teachings. Do you?"

"Yes."

"Then you must understand your decision. It is a serious one. Do you agree?"

"Yes."

"Then you have made the correct decision. When the time comes, you will know it. Until then, it would be dishonest of you to be baptized."

"My father wants me to."

"You are you. Not your father. If you need me to, I'll explain your decision to him."

I walked outside. David was sitting on the front steps of the church, waiting for his father to pick him up. "Are you doing it?" he asked.

"Nah."

"I thought so."

"Really. Why?"

"I jus' did."

"You?"

"Yes."

"I thought so too."

• • •

"So, is everything all set for this Sabbath?"
"I'm not going to do it," I said to my mother.
"Why not?"
"I don't know. It just doesn't feel right." What I really felt was anger. I wanted nothing to do with that church or the school. But I knew better than to come right out and say it.

It was not even two years ago, I was in public school, and had all my friends. Getting baptized was like surrender. I knew it would be too much for my father. Too bad. Whatever he did or said, I would not change my mind. I wouldn't argue or say anything either. It might feel good to do that, but it would only make things worse and get me too much attention. Since my father got religion, I learned very quickly to keep a low profile. I never volunteered any information, answered certain questions vaguely and with misdirection. I didn't care, if I needed to lie, I would. But this decision was like a red, hot poker in my father's eye.

"I agree with you," said my mother. "Let me talk to your father. "You can do it another time when you feel ready. I'll explain that it's a bit scary for you."

And that lie worked.

• • •

It was almost the end of the Christmas break, and I hadn't seen my best childhood friend, Mary. I lived at 99 North Main, and she was at 95, just the other side of Charlie's Bar and Grill, the place where I learned to use a floor buffer. God truly does work in mysterious ways. And as Molly Schwartz, the joint owner of the bar, told me when I was eight, "Nothing should never be a total waste." I was now the sole runner of the Adventist school's floor buffing machine. (I became the one and only polisher of floors for the whole school because no one could run the buffer without sending the machine through the wall, including the maintenance man.)

It was late Friday afternoon. I would need to go to evening worship at the church when the sun went down, but I had to see her. It was like I had been away for three months. Though I had been away for three months, we slipped right back into our old comfortableness. Then I found out that she was moving to Hawthorne, not too far away but not right next store. It was quite upsetting for me. She was the main person I went to since my father got religion and discovered that I was alive. I liked him better when he drank too much.

"When?" I asked her.

"In a couple of weeks," Mary said. "It will be so nice. Everybody will finally have their own private bedroom. There's two bathrooms, and there's a big yard for a garden."

Mary's bedroom doubled as a living room.

She, her parents, and her Aunt Nellie had been living in four small rooms since I knew her. We talked for some time about the move. She was so excited and happy. I didn't bring up anything about the school in Virginia or the baptism thing, though that was a good part of why I wanted to see her.

"Where is the house?" I asked.

"It's easy to find. Just take the number 22 bus to Hawthorne, get out by Goffle Brook Park. It's just on the other side."

She wrote down the address, but I knew that it might as well be in Asia, and that we'd never see each other again. It was time for me to go. She walked me to the front door. I stepped down the three steps to the sidewalk and turned to say goodbye. Alice, Mary's mother, appeared in the open doorway beside her daughter. She hadn't realized I was home, nor that I was in the house with Mary. She chatted a bit about their move and coming to see the new house in a few weeks. I told her I was going back to Virginia and that I'd try in the summer.

"Oh, that's right. We've been so busy with the move I forgot for a minute. How do you like it at that school?"

She and Mary looked down at me, waiting for my answer.

I felt small. It was a simple question, a simple courtesy. My response, delayed just long enough, brought a look of apprehension to their faces.

"I hate it. I don't ever want to go back."

No one spoke.

I began to cry.

Then I turned and started for home.

And that feeling has never left me. It got buried, never to see the light of day until I started to write about that world so long ago. It still hurts, but it's more like a healing wound.

6

THE LORD GIVETH AND THE LORD TAKETH AWAY

This is a story about paying attention to the details. As teenagers, we start off knowing all the right answers. But if we're lucky, life brings us to that most important question. Who am I?

I had been bobbing and weaving, ducking and slinking, even slippin' an' slidin' (a prescient poetic moment that was channeling the future Little Richard) since my return whenever I saw Pastor Milner. It was a foolishness that only delayed the inevitable— that monotonously repetitive, intrusively acidic question intent on eating away my peace of mind, which always started with him saying, "DID YOU…?"

I had arrived back at school on Sunday, so I was able to avoid the unavoidable for two days until religion class on Wednesday, which was good since most of me was out searching for the Enola Gay. It was a backsliding revival of happier childhood moments: to escape through fantasy.

I was never in a charitable mood when it came to Pastor Milner. I had had enough of his persistent pestering about my hair, my clothes, my attitude, my handy excuses. He was right about my hair, but I was no longer willing to put up with it. I was like the little kid who has been bullied and bullied and finally figured out what to do about it. Something in me had snapped during my last-minute plea to my father to let me leave Shenandoah Valley Academy, and I knew it wouldn't take much to set me off. As I entered the classroom, the Pastor said he wanted to see me directly after class. I was tired of feeling like a piece of hunted meat, so I thought I should start that day by doing some stalking of my own. How I wasn't sure, but, trusting to fate, I knew a way would present itself if I really wanted one. It was an approach that had come to my defense before. It simply meant sitting up and paying close attention. And to my amazement, something occurred in that very class.

That day's lesson was the book of Genesis. I listened to Pastor Milner's recitation of the Creation story: how God created the world in six days, rested on the seventh, that Eve was created from Adam's rib, and how we humans were given dominion over the earth, etc., etc., the usual stuff, all part of the cultural DNA found in the bloodstream of all Christian denominations with one caveat: this church's doctrinal belief in the irrefutable, literal reality of the Bible. If the Bible said six days for creation, by God it was six days. Not more. Not less. Six real twenty-four-hour days. But in my public school back in Paterson, New Jersey, thirteen miles from evil New York City, I had learned about Darwin and, of course, evolution.

"What about dinosaurs?" I asked in a plainly innocent voice.

That was an easy one. "Satan created those things to lead us astray," Milner responded very matter of factly.

What can you say to something like that? As a thirteen-year-old, nothing. He may as well have said the earth is flat, and if you go far enough west, you will fall off the edge.

But an itch to throw caution aside was eating at my guts. I sat there ruminating. *I wonder what Satan was if he could go around creating things too. Was that in the Bible? Not in the creation story, that's for sure.*

I was inching closer toward that bleak battlefield of close hand-to-hand combat but not quite willing enough to risk a direct confrontation. At least not a large one. I began looking for some small incongruity in the day's lesson to exploit and thought I found one.

So, I asked, near the end of class, since God took a rib from Adam to make Eve, did that mean men now had one less rib than women? A silly, childish question, but one that would let Milner know that the top of my head wasn't a funnel-shaped utensil made for him to dump things in. Well that was the idea. He gave me a puzzled look, then said that any questions anyone had would be addressed next class. Our assignment was to study the creation story for an in-depth discussion next class. That he would welcome a lively Christian discussion on the subject, unbelievably leaving himself wide open to my teenage impulses.

On the way out of class, Pastor Milner wanted to know, "Did you get baptized during Christmas?"

I could have lied and simply said, "Yes." But, instead, I said, "I'm sorry, Pastor Milner, but I need to get to my job. The floors haven't been cleaned for three weeks." Sometimes my impulse to lie failed me, a momentary irrational surge of ethical behavior. Admittedly it was obviously a wimpy way of sidestepping the issue. He let it pass. And I slunk away.

I ate a quick lunch, then went back to the dorm to change for work.

A few days went by, during which I split my afternoons between floor buffing and room painting. My mind was filled with the most confused thoughts. All the displeasures of my life at home and school were surging corrosively through my body, in every waking hour, even in my dreams. In one disturbing dream, I entered a dark cellar of an ancient stone structure through which I was searching for some unknown valuable object, which I was thrilled to find. But, as I made my way outside the object disappeared. I wasn't sure what it meant, but I had it often enough to realize that something was bothering me, and I had a pretty good idea what that was. I was losing touch with myself, with the real me.

Against my own better judgment, beyond my ability to control my thoughts, I now knew where this situation and I were headed. I strained to hold it off. But I couldn't.

I wanted nothing more to do with my cool-headed subterfuge to keep the adults in my life at bay. That realization actually surprised me, overwhelmed me like a sharp slap on the back of the head. I needed to do something that would relieve the pain I felt at the base of my skull.

Why don't you go for a walk?

• • •

But I didn't go on a walk. I did something better. Instead, I quickly did my floor job, asked my new roommate, Charlie, to join me, and we headed off to a cave that was in a wooded hillside at the other side of the Shenandoah River.

It was a warm afternoon that hinted at an early, sweet spring. A light snow several days before had completely melted. We crossed the tracks and headed up the slope that led to a scrubby growth that concealed the entrance. There was a thick hoarfrost around the small opening caused by moist air drifting up out of the cave. This wasn't my favorite cave. It was merely the closest and easiest to get to from school. It had been the first wild cave I explored, shortly after I arrived at Shenandoah.

As soon as we entered the cave, the snug, alternative reality began to calm me down. I had been to this particular cave at least a half dozen times. It was just ho-hum. Fun enough, but nothing special. This time, Charlie and I were going to give it a real going over. There had to be something more to it. I wanted there to be. On a molecular level, I knew the cave was a metaphor for my life at the school.

The entrance, shaped like the neck of a pastry tube, led to an area, perhaps twenty feet across and eight feet high, steeply sloped downward, which was filled with a jumble of huge rocks big enough to nearly fill the space and conceal both of us so completely from each other that we were quickly out of sound or sight as we perused our own separate searches.

The air was crisp and clean, and quite dry for a cave, which, I speculated, was the reason there were few formations: no stalagmites, no stalactites, no glistening wet walls. Just dull, dusty, red, brown, and gray stone. We continued on independently. I took my time. There seemed nothing more to be found when I noticed a small tunnel about three feet in diameter. I crawled into it only to find it ended in about five yards. I impulsively decided to lie down in a spreadeagle position, face-up on the cool earth. The tunnel was large enough at this point so that a sweeping motion of my legs and arms could not reach the walls or ceiling above. I watched my warm breath pool in the air as I lay there for a few moments, as the pressure that had brought me there faded away. I turned off my light and waited. This was not the first time I had done this. A month before, someone had dared me to do this same thing. This was after I told him how I overcame fear when I found myself stuck in a long tunnel that took me two hours to back out of.

His conditions were that I give up my flashlight and wait for him to return. And see if it didn't scare me. It didn't. Instead, I felt a surge of excitement. Instead, all thoughts and fears were replaced with a euphoric sense of wellbeing. And here I was again doing the same thing, this time self-imposed, unable to see or hear anything, feeling the cool earth and the awareness of being alive.

I don't know how long I lay there. Eventually, I went to look for my roommate.

When I found him, he told me he was sure the cave was hopelessly uninteresting, lacked any good formations, and was just jumbled rocks wherever he went. Which, of course, I knew before we left the school campus. He knew it too, though I knew I had played this visit up with a certainty that we would find something special. It may have been unfair of me to bring him here hoping for great expectations, but I had sold myself on the idea as much as he had sold himself. I couldn't believe it was such a plain-Jane-affair. That there must be a secreted heart that would be magical, and if we were careful enough in our search, we would find it.

I didn't tell him anything about my other peculiar need, the one that asked me to lie down in the dark, a need that accompanied me to every wild cave. Where could I start on such a strange need? A feeling for which there was no name.

Once I rejoined him, it took another hour of deliberate searching to reach the last room, which was quite big, about the size of a large church nave, but with a low tilting ceiling that paralleled the sloping floor. There was nothing special to be seen here either, but there were so many nooks and crannies, it was possible something undiscovered, a tunnel leading farther on, might have been missed on previous visits.

We set about scrambling into every corner with every hope of finding that great discovery. If there was such a possibility, it was here in the last room that we hoped to find it. That tunnel that would lead to an enormous, never seen cavern beyond.

More huge blocks of stone, even larger than those we encountered at the beginning, littered the floor throughout this room. Charlie went off on his own, again, while I moved down toward the extreme bottom end of the room where the floor dropped off into a fairly deep, somewhat tricky crevasse. There were several small passages led off in random directions. In order to see into some of them, I had to suspend myself upside down between stones to get a better look, but none of the passages were large enough for me to enter. This was the absolute end of the cave. The whole cave was as I remembered it: small, unusually dry, and featureless. Why had I decided that it held a secret?

I was at the bottom of the crevasse resting when Charlie called out to me, "You find anything?"

"No. Nothing's over here. "

"Let's get out of here. It's getting late," he said.

I was now on my hands and knees, looking under an enormous slab. "Just another minute. I've never looked under here before, Charlie."

I didn't wait for a reply. I turned back to the large slab, which had a narrow slit of space between itself and the rubble-covered floor. Lying on my stomach, I slithered into the compressed space. There was a tunnel hidden deep under the large rock slab. The slab must have fallen from the ceiling long ago, obscuring the tunnel, making it nearly impossible to enter. This was exciting. It's why I was there.

In the short time I had been at SVA, I had gotten a reputation among some of the boys for being a maniacal spelunker. Maybe I was. For me, it was the only thing worth doing. I'd even started to get some spelunking gear: a carbide lamp, a helmet, a large flashlight, a climbing rope, things that no one else seemed to have. I usually went with two or three other boys. Because I was small, I often went ahead to see if a passage would be passable for the others.

Here I was in a cave, every inch I had scrutinized with the hopeful fantasy it would connect into a cavern that could rival the size of the world-famous Endless Caverns in New Market, Virginia. And I had every confidence that I would be the one to find it. It was a luscious dream propelled by my need to escape my everyday existence.

As I spiraled up the ten-foot corkscrew tunnel, it became obvious that no one larger than myself could ever get through the twists and turns. As my shoulders broke free from the tunnel terminus, I brought my flashlight up to find the way forward. I was amazed at what I saw. The passage opened out into a room, maybe forty by twenty feet, too low for standing, with its' floor completely covered by exquisite starburst crystal spheres on slender four-inch crystal stems, so fragile I would not go farther for fear of destroying them. I had been in all the commercial caves in the area. Of these, I thought Luray Caverns, filled with incredible formations, was the most beautiful but never had I seen anything equal to what lay before me. How can I describe what I felt? It was beyond any rude boyhood adventure I had ever known. Not for its thrilling danger but because of its beauty – totally unexpected in that unadorned cave. Made more intense because of it. It was a feeling of joy and giddiness that filled every bit of me as I lay there not one arms-length from that weightless crystal universe.

Charlie must have worked his way toward me, for I heard him calling, "Where are you? It's nearly time for dinner."

Only the top third of my body had made it into the room. As I pushed against the carpeted floor of the room to back down the tunnel, a small heart-shaped chunk the size of a teacup broke free with a small forest of crystals standing proud upon it. I picked it up and whispered, "Thank you."

When I finally wriggled out of the tunnel, my roommate was waiting for me. I described what I found and showed him the small heart-shaped rock, but it didn't seem to mean much to him, which I understood. He looked under the rock slab that began the tunnel and saw it was too small and contorted for him to ever get through to the room.

With barely enough time left to get back to the school and get cleaned up for dinner, we scrambled quickly out of the cave.

How different our two visits were: for him, disappointing, For me, not what I had hoped for. Much, much more.

The next day, nothing existed for me: not my classes, nor my lunch which I gobbled down, my job, which I ignored, or anything to do with that place or anyone else in it. Nothing existed but the need to get back to the cave as quickly as possible.

I'm Not Here

Not a wise thing to do, I went by myself.

Knowing the cave as well as I did, I found my way back through the tortuous course to the large room quickly. I scrambled down through its chunky rock-strewn surface to the slab of rock and the corkscrew tunnel.

I couldn't find it. I went back and started my exploration of the large room again. I could not find it.

I tried several more times, searching meticulously for perhaps an hour. Crawling and climbing over a jumble of large rock slabs until I was frantic, confused, and exhausted. It's easy to become disoriented in a cave. And I was sure that was what had happened to me, though I prided myself on never having had that problem before. At last, I stopped to rest, and to look about. It was only then I realized that a large part of the room was literally unrecognizable. And then I knew, as an explosion of fear overwhelmed me, that sometime between yesterday afternoon and that afternoon, in less than twenty-four hours, a large portion of the roof had collapsed. I sat there trying to absorb what my body already knew. That neither I nor anyone else would ever see that crystalline world again, nor ever feel what I felt the day before. Had the roof fallen during the night, or this morning, maybe ten minutes after I left the cave? There was no sign of it having just occurred. So, it was yesterday.

"You could have died," I said aloud, as if someone else were chastising me for my foolishness.

In the past, I never paid any attention, but there were rocks falling all the time in this cave, every time—rocks falling—sounding small in size but clear warnings, had I cared to pay attention. Panic ricocheted through my body, stuck in my throat, compressed my hands around my face. I had to get out.

Sitting at my desk, back in my other world, I sensed that that experience had some sort of connection to my life at the school. That room. It was just too powerful. The heart-shaped stone sat on my desk. Why should I make such a connection? Should I return the stone to the cave? It felt like a theft.

During the whole time I was having this conversation with myself, I was working on the assignment for my religion class when I asked myself why was this school so scary and my laying in the pitch-blackness of the cave not at all?

I'm not sure how long after that realization, I found I was back in my religion class listening to my classmates' rote responses to questions they had most likely responded to in the same way many times before. I, too, had learned to mimic the same responses in just a few short years. Yes, the world was created in six days, and Eve was made from Adam's rib, and the one and only God had created man in his own image. Except I couldn't accept any of it because it seemed so improbable. Was I the only one in this classroom to not accept this story as the literal truth? Why couldn't I? Why couldn't I just accept it and get on with the rest of the day? I'd gone to church, at least some church if not this one, my entire life. I knew the story. Why now did I find it incomprehensible? Something had happened to me. But why did the cave have a connection to these thoughts? It, too, made no sense. But, in the back of my confused mind, on a misty level, something was trying to emerge.

Over the next few days, I gave some serious study time to my religion class to the exclusion of other coursework. The first such serious effort for any subject since I left seventh grade. I decided to read the book of Genesis carefully. And I was amazed to discover there were two differing versions of the creation story in that same book. Two. Right there in the King James Bible. Why were there two versions? Two completely contradictory versions as well. I'd never heard of such a thing. There wasn't any mention of this in any church or class or sermon I'd ever heard of before. Now I was just plain curious. What began as ordinary teenage contrariness in my silly feud with Milner had now become a puzzlement. In the version I had encountered all my young life, God created the universe in six days and rested upon the seventh. That version was the linchpin of the Adventist

Church, was a significant part of the reason for their going to church on Saturday instead of Sunday.

In the second Biblical version, everything was created in one day, without resting. Which made partial sense to me because I couldn't imagine God needing to rest ever. He was God!

Back in the first version, God created man and women in his image at the same time with no mention of Adam's rib being used, which made me wonder what God naked might look like, a perverse diversion in my thoughts that I tried to dispel so as not to be struck by a bolt of lightning. But in the second version, Adam's rib is used to create Eve, which means Adam must have been created before her.

It took me a bit of time to work up the courage, but in the next class, I asked the Pastor, in all sincerity, to explain the discrepancies between the two creation stories. "Why would God need to rest, Pastor Milner? Does he get tired too like us?" That was where the main difficulty lay for me. "Which one should I believe?" I asked.

I watched his face go white. And for once, he went momentarily silent, which shocked me. I can't recall how, but in some way, the question was circumvented, and the class moved on while my mind, having lost interest in the Q and A process, drifted off to thoughts about the roof of the cave collapsing without warning.

As I wrote this story, I remembered that upon leaving class, I unexpectedly and immediately realized for the first time there were literal and convincingly good reasons to not believe any of what Pastor Milner said. In that moment, what I had done stopped being about the religion, the school, or my father, about the game of getting even. It was about me. As I walked down the porch stairs of the administration building, a rush of heat flashed through me, and I felt weak. It was fear. And I had done it to myself.

At this point in my life, I felt as though I had drifted aloft. Not a state of light, airy ecstasy, but untethered, with no idea how far down "down" was.

When you're a teenager, the best way to prepare for adult life is to have as much pointless lunacy, for which no reasonable explanation can be found, crammed into your life in the shortest period of time possible.

7

Burma Shave

Things, for no apparent reason, had quieted down—like the notes in my underwear from the girls in the laundry about my cuteness. The senior boys never again grabbed me from the shower or held me by my feet, stark naked, from the third-floor bathroom window for their amusement and the girls hanging up laundry below.

In the meantime, the senior boys went off terrorizing some other freshmen I supposed. At least a momentary reduction of terror in my life. Which meant I could take showers again. Then for some reason, a boy named Gerry walked up to me one day and said, "I don't want you near my sister."

First of all, I had no idea who his sister was. Until that pronouncement, I had little to no awareness of Gerry's existence. I knew him only by the size of his bulging muscles. He was part of a cadre of obsessive weightlifters that dominated the first-floor boys lounge every day. Second of all, I could have reminded him of the thirty-six-inch rule of separation. In no way could I be near whoever his sister was without bringing down the wrath of the entire power structure of the school.

There was only one girl I was talking to, really talking to, having conversations with. Her name was Connie. Connie was his sister. I didn't know that, and she hadn't told me. He never used her name, and I wasn't brave enough to have a long enough chat with him to ask that question?

"Is Gerry your brother?"

"Is he bothering you?"

"Sort of."

"Did he threaten you?"

"Sort of."

"He is a pain. Just ignore him."

"I'm not so sure, Connie. Why's he like that?"

"He thinks it's his job as my big brother."

Okay. So, I guess Gerry didn't like me talking to his sister. However, Connie, unlike her overbearing brother, was outgoing and very, very pretty. Simply easy to talk to despite the school's rule of separation. I wasn't interested in having a girlfriend at the moment nor, she a boyfriend. But someone that didn't think I had two heads was refreshing for the moment.

Her weightlifting brother never touched me, but he did continue to mumble terrifying threats about ending my life. I ignored him. Human warmth, at any cost, was worth his palpable threats of death.

Then, out of the blue, Onko, the laconic American Indian (he had no second name that I know of), walked up to me while I was cleaning the hall floor in the classroom building. He suddenly appeared out of thin air in front of the buffing machine, so suddenly it was all I could do not to run him over.

"Do you like baked potatoes?" He had a deep, resonant voice.

"Yes?" I said, not questioningly but confused. My mind had been elsewhere, possibly on Mars, while I, on autopilot, was buffing the floor.

"Don't go to dinner tonight."

Don't go to dinner tonight? Is that what he said?

"Meet me out by the pond."

I shook my head yes, and he was gone. Onko was the giant senior boy that had held me out the third-floor window by my heels.

Should I go? Maybe it's a return of the senior terror squad using subterfuge to threaten my life again? Don't go to dinner tonight Jerry, sounds like a trap.

I decided not to meet him.

I'm Not Here

• • •

Another thing that had quieted down was the oppressive atmosphere of the boys' dorm, coinciding with the arrival of the new boy's dean. Dean Feder was asked to leave when it was discovered he liked boys too much.

Dean Reilly was really a nice man. Strict, but very fair. That made one less thing to worry about. It was rumored that he had been a Marine. Strange to understand since Adventists were always conscientious objectors: they wouldn't carry or fire a weapon. It didn't matter, Marine or not, I liked him.

He also pronounced my name correctly and always did.

• • •

The pesky senior girls finally got bored with my reluctance to follow their romantic plans for my life. And while they were not as unpleasant as Pastor Milner, they were closely related in their meddlesome need to force their will upon me. They couldn't resist my four-foot ten-inch cuteness, drawn to their attention by my dangling from the third-floor bathroom window. So, they attempted to pair me up with petite four-foot-eight Josephine in order to show those senior boys their scheme to embarrass me didn't work.

• • •

It was delusional, but for a brief moment, I thought Pastor Milner finally gave up on me. I had become a classic rebellious teenager where he was concerned, needling him whenever he came near. I seldom got through his class without saying something sarcastic or contrary. I know he put a note or two in my file about my behavior and let the dean know how unsuited I was to be at their school, even a threat to the other students' perfection of their Christian lives. But I couldn't resist the pleasurable surge of pure joy I felt whenever I succeeded in making him infuriated, which was easy since he was so unable to see beyond his cubical version of reality. One day on the way out of class, another student asked why I hated Pastor Milner so much. We had reached the door where the Pastor always posted himself.

"No. No," I said loud enough for him to hear, "he's not important enough to hate. It's just so easy to get a rise out of him. I can't resist. It's just for fun."

It's embarrassing to admit, but there is still enough of that teenager left in me that I still enjoy that memory. No. I'm not embarrassed. This attitude alone, according to some of my New Age friends, is enough to have me return as a bug in my next life. But in my opinion, life offers us few moments of victory over the vicissitudes of Milner types to be squandered on feelings of remorse or guilt. Maybe I'll be a grasshopper.

. . .

My grades were just beginning to slide in a negative direction. I suppose because of my generally confused mental state, I wasn't studying. Up until then, I didn't need to because the course work still hadn't caught up to the level of my seventh-grade class instruction back in public school. I was managing a "B" average without studying, even in Spanish. My grade in religion class was closer to a C, though I always did well on quizzes. I thought I deserved an +A just for my creative contrarian comments.

There were other assorted things that still were prickly, but by and large, the major issues had truly quieted down.

At supper time, I was surprised to find myself out at the pond searching for Onko. It had shadings of a 'B' horror film, where, against your better judgment, you have left a warm, cozy, well-lit room to see what caused that horrific sound in the rainy darkness outside the house.

I'm Not Here

The sky was overcast, nearly dark, the air cold, uncomfortably close, and threatening rain. At first, I didn't see him. The pond was not very large, so I thought he wasn't there, or perhaps he and the other senior boys were hiding in a wooded area on the far side of the pond. Reluctantly, I worked my way around toward the trees. Nestled in a small cleared spot among the scrubby undergrowth, I saw Onko sitting on a log by a small fire. He looked up at me but said nothing, then motioned for me to join him on the log.

What's this about? I wondered. *Are there boys waiting for me to get settled, only to then sneak up on me in the dark?*

He poked at the wood coals with a stick.

How was he able to do this, have a fire? What if we were seen? Weren't we visible? We were sure to be caught, get in trouble.

There was something about this situation that held me in place. I didn't say anything. He kept prodding the fire. Several more minutes passed in silence. Then, with a knowing movement, he maneuvered two foil-wrapped potatoes from the fire. He unwrapped them and handed one to me. He didn't seem to notice the heat as I juggled mine from hand to hand. He indicated that I hold the potato with my fingertips, shifting among them as they got too hot. We ate in silence. And when we were both finished, he covered the fire coals with earth, stood, and walked away into the darkness.

It was several years, really, many years, before I understood what that evening was about. He was sorry for what he had done. And all these years later, I love him for that honest kindnesses.

I had turned thirteen in February, the age at which, in many world cultures, you transition into the adult world. I still wanted to play boy games. One warm spring day, Cassie Teal and I, at his suggestion, were playing guns — running from tree to tree, falling down occasionally in the traditionally feigned throes of an agonizing death. We were savvy enough to play behind the classroom building, out of sight of the dorms, but didn't realize we had strayed into the yard of the school principal's house.

It was my turn to die because Cassie had successfully ambushed me. As I collapsed in exquisite pain upon the ground, we heard a screen door slam and a woman's voice call out to us. Cassie turned and ran for cover while I struggled to right myself. A slender woman, perhaps in her fifties, clad in a house dress and bib apron, put down her basket of laundry and walked toward me. She was wearing wire frame glasses, her wispy salt and pepper hair clasped in a bun at the nape of her neck.

"Hello. I'm Mrs. Beiber. What's your name?"

"Jerry."

"Who was the other boy?"

I didn't want to tell her.

"Do you know? Don't the both of you go to school here?"

"Yes."

"Are you afraid?"

"I guess."

"There's no need. Would you like a piece of pie?"

"Are we in trouble?"

"Does a piece of apple pie sound like trouble to you? Come on in the house. I made it this morning. It should be cool by now. How 'bout a glass of milk too?"

I followed her into the kitchen. We both sat down at the table. She watched me as I ate the pie, manna from heaven.

"Where are you from?"

"Paterson, New Jersey."

"Isn't that near New York City?"

That alone endeared her to me. We talked on for nearly an hour, about my life up north, and there at school, trying not to reveal my negative attitudes. After all, I was eating her pie. As I rose to leave, she said, "I make pie every Tuesday. Next week it will be peach. Do you like peach?"

I shook my head yes. She was the first person since I had been at that school that treated me with kindness instead of suspicion. She talked to me the way Molly Schwartz, my grownup friend did back home, with interest and a genuine smile on her face.

"Is that a maybe or a yes?"

"It's a yes. Thank you."

"Next Tuesday then?"

"Yes." And I went there often on Tuesdays for the rest of the year. I kept it to myself. Except I did tell Cassie what he missed, but he never joined me. Otherwise, I keep it secret. But, like so many other things in my life, I didn't want that perfection intruded upon. Not a very sharing attitude, but then, I doubted anyone else would be interested.

· · ·

It was time for our spring Easter vacation: one of those pagan / Christian holidays, which in my contrarian mental state, I knew to be a mix of oversexed rabbits and the resurrection of the son of God, united by a basket of brightly dyed eggs, a ham dinner, cheap candy, and a waxy chocolate bunny. (Due to Adventism, the ham dinner was now a walnut roast.)

· · ·

At the last possible moment, the travel money arrived, which I pocketed, and at the age of thirteen, with nary a moment's hesitation, made the intelligent decision to hitchhike home three hundred thirty-one miles for the second time that year. My first ride, in a new 1953 Chevrolet, left me gasping for air near Winchester after a headlong devil-may-care ride. It seemed the cars' owner of one day was intent on testing the four-door Chevy's capacities.

I had started this ride in the front passenger seat.

"God'am. God'am it. Shit. Shit, shit, shit," he said more than audibly to himself.

I looked at him in a stunned state of recollection at those once-familiar words. (From my early childhood, of course.)

"Fucking piece of shit."

Fucking, it was understood, was not acceptable among my friends before the age of eleven. "Is there something wrong?" I offered tentatively.

"WHAT?"

"Are you upset?"

"Damn straight."

I thought that the scenery might be flashing by a tad too quickly. Up ahead, I could see our approach to a series of Burma Shave signs, ubiquitous along major southern roadways then. The Burma Shave company, in a clever campaign to promote its product, erected a series of six signs, spaced equal distance apart to be read as you drove down the road, usually humorous, and unavoidable in their commercial intent.

They were coming up fast.

Every shave / now can sno… / six more min… / than bef…/ by using /… And of course, the last one was always Burma Shave.

"How fast are we going?"

"WHAT?"

"I couldn't read those signs." We were heading down a long hill.

"This God'am car. I'm not goanna' quit till I hits a hun'ert."

"How fast we goin' now?"

"Ninety-eight."

"You mind if I climb into the back? I'm tired, and I need a nap." Without waiting for his answer, I climbed over the seat.

"Even down this God'am hill, this shit bucket won't make it."

I slithered down onto the floor of the car for safety while thoughts about a nice relaxed bus ride to D.C. whizzed through my mind as I waited for the crash to occur.

• • •

"How are things going, son?"

Since my father had gotten religion, his whole personality had taken on a new cast. Leprous. Never before had he referred to me as "son." It felt like a scene from Father Knows Best, a popular radio show then.

Fresh from my more forceful personality début in religion class, I said, "I hate it down there and I'm not going back next year. I want to go to a different school." This was, no doubt, a repeat of my Thanksgiving message, but with a more assertive tone.

He and I were locked in a staring contest. My mother turned around from her kitchen chores but remained nervously silent.

Devoid of his dismissive claims of my homesickness, it was a repeat of our Thanksgiving blowup, but it went no further. He seemed to avoid the issue, which I read as a partial victory, but it left the air filled with a hovering anger that permeated the rest of my visit.

I spent the rest of the Christmas break doing solitary things: jigsaw puzzles, building a model fighter jet, sneaking off to the movies. One afternoon between the holidays, I dug my hand-painted lead Knights in Armor and a large box of plastic bricks out of the back of my closet. I went outside in the backyard and built a large castle with all the soldiers in it. I then built a small catapult from some twigs, string, a plastic spoon, and a rubber band, which I used to fling lit birthday candles into the fort. It took most of the afternoon, but I succeeded in burning the whole affair into a puddle of molten lead and black goo. It was my own impromptu rite of passage without full immersion in a tank of water.

Hello, I must be going.

8

He's Bad News

Maybe there should be at least one moment in your life when you can look back with pride at a significant accomplishment that occurred just because of your action, at just the right moment, that saved the day.

Even when there's no anesthetic, a swig of whiskey, or a stick to bite on, things will work out just fine if you pick yourself up, dust yourself off and start all over again.

Mr. Reilly, the boy's dean, surprised everyone by organizing a camp out for all the boys up in The Blue Ridge Mountains, the other side of New Market. We left after classes on Friday, caravanned to a remote site, hiked a good distance into the forest, and set up camp. The sun was nearly down. We had eaten dinner and were sitting around a large campfire telling stories. This was an exciting treat, never having camped out before.

My roommate and I had set up our sleeping gear a good distance away from the campfire. It was nearly dark when I realized I'd need my flashlight to get back to my bedroll. Not wanting to miss anything, I took off at a good clip to get the light. I slipped on some wet autumn leaves, did a complete somersault, and came down on a rock with my right knee. Unable to get up, I yelled for help. I had split my knee open, and it was bleeding profusely.

Eventually, Herbie came looking for me. "Did you fall?"

Ignoring his question, I asked, "Did I miss anything, Herbie?"

"Like what?"

"Toasting marshmallows?" Why had I asked about something so silly? I hated marshmallows toasted or otherwise.

"Toasting marshmallows! They'd never let us have marshmallows. What's wrong with you?"

"Well, I just thought—"

"Gosh! Look at all the blood. Can you get up? Umm, I guess not. I better get help."

With Dean Reilly and some of the boys helping, I made it back to his car. He was not happy. It meant he needed to leave the boys on their own while he took me to see Dr. Parrot back in New Market. The village doctor took care of any serious problems for the school.

We arrived at his house shortly before sundown. The doctor seemed unhappy about our disturbing presence and the amount of blood I was depositing on everything as I hopped into his office, which looked like something out of Oliver Twist. There were shelves to the ceiling stuffed with dust-covered equipment and supplies, a ceiling fixture of bare light bulbs, and a window caked with prehistoric grim. He and the dean helped me up onto his examination table. I lay propped up on my elbows as he cut my pants away. Up until that point, he was uninterested and impatient with my presence.

"My! My! My! Ya'll did a magnificent job of it. Magnificent."

For the first time, I took a look, and I had to agree. I'd never seen one of my own bones before. It seemed like a privilege to get a look at this unknowable part of me, rather like meeting a shy stranger that shared my existence in secret. That detached speculation ended abruptly, though, when he started poking around.

"Might be good to get y'all ta' hospital." He took a deep, focusing breath. Pursed his lips speculatively and said, "Don't think anything is broken. Does this hurt?"

He twisted my leg from side to side.

Of course, it hurt. That was right up there with Herbie's question, "Did you fall down?"

No, I'm just resting, Herbie.

"How 'bout this? That Hurt?"

"Not too much," I lied

He was a man in his sixties. He looked like we had gotten him out of a deep sleep at seven-thirty.

"That'd be too much hassle for ever'a'body," talking to himself. "Ah, 'en goin' ta' hospital. And keep Mr. Reilly from getting' back. Too much trouble fer ever'a'body," he continued to mutter to himself. "Think I'll just sew y'all up here."

The cut was actually a jagged four-inch tear that meandered off in several directions across the top of my knee.

He went to get his equipment. When he came back, he looked at me and said, "Couldn't find any anesthetic. Believe I'm out."

My mind flashed on some old movies from my heathen past life—when movies were a part of it—where the hero, me in this case, would be given a swig of whiskey and a stick to bite on.

"We'll have to do this the old fashion way. You're a boy. You can take it. Ya wanna watch? Be good for y'all. Why don't ya sit up again?"

Naturally, I didn't want to look like a sissy, so I unhappily sat up to watch. Actually, it distracted me from some of the pain. A half hour-later, the last stitch went in.

"Now ya know, ya'll can't bend your leg 'til it heals. Y'all 'll pull the stitches out. If ya don't want a nasty scar, don't bend your leg."

"How long will that take?"

'Mmmm, two, three weeks."

I struggled off his operating table, got to the car, and slowly bent my knee enough to fit in the dean's two-door Plymouth Coupe.

• • •

I'm Not Here

The dean took me back to school, told me I was on my own. No one would be back in the dorm 'til Sunday. Of course, he added, "And stay out of trouble." Which didn't seem like much of a challenge under the circumstances.

Saturday morning, I looked at my knee. Most of the stitches had torn out during the night. I went down to the dorm office, found the first aid kit, taped thin strips across the wound as best as I could to pull it together, and put a new dressing on it. Then I hobbled outside to sit on the front porch in the sun. I limped onto the masonry buttress alongside the steps, stretched my wounded leg straight out, leaned back against the large colonial column, and closed my eyes.

"Hey, Jerry. What y'all doin'? Why aren't ya campin' out with all the other boys?"

The source of the voice seemed to be coming from a shadowy silhouette of a girl under the trees. Girls rarely came to this part of the campus. *Very peculiar*, I thought.

"I got hurt."

She emerged into the sunlight at the foot of the stairs. She looked familiar but I couldn't place her. There didn't appear to be any faculty members about. There was some activity over at the girl's dorm. "What's goin' on over there?"

She brazenly walked up the steps and sat down next to me, then leaned back against the column and my right shoulder. "Parents' weekend for the girls."

"Are your parents here?"

"No. I live close by. My mother can come here anytime."

"How come you don't live at home then?"

"Too far for that. What happened to you?"

"Mashed up my knee. I'm not s'ppose ta use it." I shifted a little, so I could see her face.

I'd never noticed her before.

"What's your name?" There seemed to be a pleasant tingle in that shared shoulder.

"Pat Knupp."

"You new here?"

"No. I'm a Junior like you," she said through a silly grin.

I wondered what the grin was about. "How you know my name?"

"I work in the laundry." She didn't offer any more information except an even broader grin.

"The laundry?"

"It's my third year there."

"Oh. OH! I guess you saw me?" It was one of those questions you already knew the answer to. Meaning she was one of the girls that saw me naked, hanging from the third story window two years before.

"Oh, yes. Every bit of ya'll. It's somethin' I'll never forget."

A warm redness flashed across my face, and then I had a sudden realization. "It was you, wasn't it?" We both moved enough to glimpse each other.

"Me? What?" the grin so strong, she was barely able to speak.

It was a nice grin. Wide-eyed, impish, and playful. "You were the one."

"I was... what?"

"Put those notes in my underwear."

"You were such a cute little boy. Even upside down."

"I stopped sending my underwear to the laundry because of you. What a pain. I had to wash them by hand myself."

"Well, I guess I did go on a mite too long." She moved back closer to me and leaned against the column.

Before the thought could form in my critical mind, I asked, "You wanna go out next Saturday night?"

"I always go out."

"I mean do you have a date? Are you going steady or sumpthin?" My face reddened again. *Maybe she still thinks of me as a little boy.* "I'm taller now," I added, thinking that might matter.

"That's nice. No, I..." she started.

"Well, what do you two think you're doing?"

She jumped up. It was Pastor Milner.

Glaring up at me he asked, "What are you doing here? Why aren't you at the camp out?"

"I got hurt."

"You've always got to be different. Don't you? Probably faking it."

"I smashed up my knee. Had to go see that old bird, Dr. Parrot, for stitches." I had to chuckle over that one. He was an old crusty bird.

"That's disrespectful."

"He nearly killed me, and he made me watch while he tried to do me in. Didn't use anything to kill the pain either!"

The trouble with you, *Mr. Vice*, you're always trying to do things your way. I'm on to you." He turned toward Pat. "You know the thirty-six-inch rule, don't you, young lady?"

"He was havin' a hard time walkin'. I jus' stopped to see if he needed help getting up the steps."

I liked her before, but now that she was lying, I really liked her. I wondered if Milner would buy it.

"Get back to your dorm. And stay away from him; he's bad news."

She stood up to leave but didn't go. We looked at each other. It was the first time in my life that everything else melted away because I was looking at a girl. And she was looking back too.

"Let's see this terrible wound, Mr. Vice."

He was still calling me vice. I responded, "My name is pronounced Vis, as in kiss. Not vice. Vis, not vice." *You idiot* was definitely in my tone.

Pat made an oh-well face, shrugged the shoulder that spoke volumes to me, and left.

"Typical teen behavior, changing the subject. Just show me."

"I can't show you out here without taking down my pants. Ya' want me ta do that?" I was on my feet at this point, had the buckle open, ready to pull them down.

"You're really good at getting around things, aren't you? Get inside and stay there. I don't want to see you again the rest of the weekend."

. . .

Friday afternoon was when clean laundry was returned to the dorms. Mine, once again, included a note in my underwear. It simply said, "Okay."

During my freshman year, I hadn't had a single real date. I was truly that little boy Pat remembered. Then came the sea change when the juices of life began to flow. In a benevolent act on my behalf, unsolicited, I might add, the senior girls contrived an act of revenge upon the senior boys for hanging me headfirst out the third-floor window of the boy's dorm, stark naked for all the laundry workers below to ogle. This revenge consisted of pairing me up with petite Josephine as my steady girlfriend, just to show the senior boys that I wasn't embarrassed, and despite their evilness, I now had a certain cachet with the opposite sex. It took Josephine and me two months to work our way out of that madness. Josephine engineered the whole thing and steered me through it all to the bitter end. Other than this lunacy, I spent most Saturday nights in the dorm. Wasn't really interested in girls. Then briefly, there was Doris. Doris and I went to the same church, back in Paterson. Two years before, at the age of eleven, Doris and I spent one afternoon sitting on my living room sofa holding hands while my mother made cookies for us in the kitchen. For a brief moment, I thought a priori that constituted a right of access to her heart. I needed something to do. But now. Now there was Pat. Maybe.

. . .

I'm Not Here

As long as the weather was relatively mild, Saturday night socials, as they were known, were held outside, behind the girl's dorm on a large concrete slab.

In 1954 Chuck Berry, Bill Haley and the Comets, Fats Domino, and so many more were sweeping the likes of Rosemary Clooney, Doris Day, and Perry Como out of the way back north. Fats Domino's Ain't That A Shame was absolutely my favorite. It was still a toss-up out there in the wider world between Rock 'n' Roll and dreary old-style pop music, but I knew in this cloistered world that the likes of Perry Como wouldn't make it over the wall, let alone Fats. Only brass band marching music was acceptable for our Saturday nights.

Strangely inconsistent with the general tenor of things, Hollywood movies did make up an occasional Saturday night social with enforced segregated seating. This was another one of those things like the camp out that seemed to thumb a nose at the rules. The two deans made those film selections. I asked Mr. Reilly why it was all right to show movies. "Isn't it wrong to see a movie?"

"No, not if it's a wholesome movie. It's seeing it in a theater. That's the problem."

"I don't understand, Mr. Reilly."

"You wouldn't want to be found there if Christ came back to earth to gather the righteous to heaven, would you?"

"So is it all right if I watch one on television then at home?" I'd heard this theater prohibition before but never took it to that next step. I wasn't trying to be clever, but I could tell from the look on his face that I had been.

As I sat on my bed reading Pat's, "OK," my mind fantasized that this first date would take place when there was a movie social and that Pat and I would sit together, in the dark.

But no. That week's Saturday night social met out on the concrete slab, a touch chilly, accompanied by – not Fats Domino, not even Grand Ole' Opry music—but the same old scratched recorded marches of John Phillip Susa played on a portable record player, set up on a folding chair, directed by a teacher with the yardstick of separation tattooed on their brain. These marches of callisthenic maneuvers consisted of intertwining, over and under, rhythmic militaristic tramping, sending boys one way, girls another, in a vague reference to square dancing, which I had learned to do in my seventh-grade gym class back in public school. The result being, you only got fleeting glimpses of your date, with occasional eyes straight ahead, side by side shuffling as the separated gender loops passed each other briefly like ships in the night longing for a collision.

After I returned from the evening merriment, my roommate, who had spent the evening productively swatting flies in our room, asked how my date went.

"I don't know. You know what these socials are like. They should change the name to un-socials." I asked, "How many flies did you get?"

"At least a hundred."

I should explain that the fly problem was amazingly out of control in my opinion and Herbie's too. As two North Jersey urban boys, the appearance of a fly, a rare occurrence in our homes, always aroused panic among all the grown-ups. It was one of my tasks as a boy to devote a whole afternoon, if necessary, to hunt one down. It was a standard held high in our home, my mother being the primary family upholder and one with which I had grown not only accustomed to but considered it to be the norm in the world. That was before I landed at SVA. Upon my arrival, I could tell immediately that this was not Paterson, New Jersey, and so I set about adjusting my notion of what to expect when I looked out my dorm room window in the morning. What I didn't, couldn't, and wouldn't adjust to were the dozen or more saucer-sized clumps of flies that gathered on the ceiling every night. As soon as there was a chill in the air, the flies would appear no matter what precautions were taken to exclude them. It became my knee-jerk behavior to walk around my room bent over as if I had just departed from a helicopter. Herbie and I took this situation very seriously and worked on a solution with diligence. There was no solving the problem permanently since the root of the problem was the school dairy farm's manure piles. What we did instead was to develop a weapon that would kill on a mass scale. Today we would have called our solution a weapon of mass destruction. Then we simply called it the swatting machine, which consisted of holding a heavy textbook, usually from the class that we held in low regard, in the palm of our hand, waist-high to give enough distance to throw the tome flat against the ceiling, usually killing about half of a saucer size gathering. So, Herbie saying that he had killed about a hundred flies meant his heart wasn't in it. Thus, I concluded we had both achieved the same level of gratification for the evening.

. . .

Since returning to SVA from my trip home to be baptized, I had revived my escapist activities with a vengeance. Though I had obtained a veneer of adventist rectitude, I still needed my country meanders to escape the pernicious atmosphere of the school. It seems baptism wasn't a cure-all for everything.

Big Mack Cave was on the other side of the river. The last time I had been there, I'd gone into a small tunnel off the main room that took fifteen minutes to reach its end and two hours to back out. I felt both lucky to be alive and stupid for doing it. This time I had no such intention. This was just meant to be a quick visit on a short Friday afternoon walk. I had to get back to shower and change for dinner and Sabbath sundown services. My new strategy to avoid being hung out the window by Seniors was to take showers when most other boys showered. It meant I'd have to endure teasing about my still hairless state, humiliating, but by comparison, a survivable condition.

Herbie decided to go with me because he had never been to that cave and he had nothing better to do.

It was a brilliantly sunny day. So, it took several minutes for our eyes to adjust to the darkness. It was an effortless entrance. Every other cave I'd been in was an instant mystery of resistance that began at the very entrance. It was this cave's singularly unique feature. The entry was at least fifteen feet high and ten or more wide, which led you into a voluminous room that was approached from the gentle bank of the Shenandoah River. After that, there was nothing much to do but experience the soothing magic of the nether world on the body and soul.

We stopped a few paces into the cave to let our eyes adjust to the dim light reaching us from the entry.

"Something's different," I said.

Herbie looked puzzled. "What's different? I don't see anything."

"It's the walls. They don't look right."

As he began to ask how I realized they looked strangely smooth. This cave hadn't any typical cave formations. Instead, the walls were roughly pock-marked with thousands of small cup-sized depressions.

"They're smooth. Everywhere. The holes are all filled in." This single room, shaped like the interior of a large church, receded out of sight in the darkness. I stepped closer and began to reach out to touch the surface of the walls, then jumped away.

"It's bats. Look. Every nook is filled with little brown bats, Herbie."

There were thousands, tens, no, hundreds of thousands of bats crammed into every possible place. Wherever we shined our lights, up to the vaulted ceiling, back into the darkness, everywhere, there were bats. I got up the nerve to pluck one out of its cavity. It didn't respond. It lay there in my hand. "They're cold-blooded." said Herb. "They can't move till they warm up."

"Yeah, your right."

"I've got an idea," he said.

And it was a great idea. A really great idea. This cave visit suddenly took on a new direction. I had a large flashlight with me that held six batteries. I dumped out the batteries, and we started plucking bats off the wall to fill the flashlight. After collecting ten mouse-sized bats, I screwed the bottom back on the flashlight. We didn't say anything to each other. We just exchanged big smiles, then left for school. An hour and a half later, we were finishing up dinner, and I was walking back to the dorm to finish dressing for the Friday night service in the school auditorium. Pastor Milner, as usual, was handling the service. There were some announcements, we sang several hymns, and then everyone bowed their heads and closed their eyes as Milner began one of his interminable prayers, thanking God for everything from the weather (regardless of what it might be) to the miraculous diminution of teenage acne. Other than a few boys around me, everybody else was well behaved with their heads still bowed, eyes closed. I fished the flashlight out from my inside coat pocket. By now, the warmth of my body had raised the occupants in the flashlight to a fevered pitch of activity. I laid a hymnal spread eagle on my lap, unscrewed the bottom cap, and dumped the frenetic creatures out on the book. I then held the hymnal flat open above my head and thrust the bats aloft, at which point Pastor Milner was only halfway through his meticulous beseeching of the deity to subdue the raging hormones of those assembled in his name.

Ten frenzied bats began swooping through the room. I screwed the flashlight back together, put it inside my coat, replaced the hymnal in the rack, and bowed my head in a feint of guilelessness. Not one snicker did I allow myself. Bats generally make no humanly audible sound, so it took a few moments until those few kids cheating on closed eyes saw them and, irrespective of Milner's uncompleted prayer checklist, let out a chorus of screams.

The room erupted in total pandemonium. The girls were the first to react to the dive-bombing bats. High pitched squeals, thrashing arms, and even the bare legs of upended girls greeted the astonished eyes of Pastor Milner. Hymnals, anything that came to hand, on the girl's side of the auditorium were thrown into the air. Some girls were standing on their seats screaming, waving the bats away from their heads, others cowered on the floor. A dozen panicked girls started running pointlessly up and down the aisles.

The boys, behaving just as you or I would have them do, jumped to their feet and were yelling and laughing themselves to tears. Some were even trying to snag a bat, all in an enormous cathartic release of pulsating joy. I stood quietly and demurely, luxuriating in the depth and breadth of my accomplishment.

At last, someone thought to charge the double rear door. The girls were the first to explode out of the building, followed by the whooping, cheering boys gasping for air. Pastor Milner, still standing at the pulpit, declared the just started meeting over to a near-empty room.

The next morning, the entire school, including the staff, were called to a joint morning prayer meeting in the same auditorium. The bats were gone, serenity and hymnals restored to their rightful place. After a truncated service, Pres. Bieber stood and informed everyone that he wanted the person responsible for last night's travesty to be identified. If that person was not pointed out, the entire school would be punished. We had until the end of Sabbath Church service to identify that person. No one spoke. We left for breakfast. A number of boys knew I was the culprit. And I was sure the number had grown overnight. I was mildly apprehensive, but the atmosphere around me as we entered the dining room was quite normal. I thought, perhaps even a tad more respectful toward me in some quarters.

Breakfast, too, was normal though filled with talk about last nights' events. Still, no one mentioned anything about finding out who did it. We were back in church an hour later. It was a quiet, sober bunch of kids that filed into the building, except for me. Outwardly I was calm; inside I was filled with spastic butterflies. The service began with the usual: an opening prayer, a hymn, and some announcements for the day. It was followed by a remarkably short, perfunctory sermon by Milner. Then President Beiber replaced the pastor at the pulpit. He then stepped away, clasped his hands behind his back, spread his legs slightly, and stood there for several minutes without speaking, just looking about the room of seated students and school staff. No one moved.

"I am disappointed to tell you that no one has come forth to tell me who is responsible for last night's disgraceful, disrespectful spectacle."

There was a long pause with no response.

"I want that information now."

There was another long pause with no response.

Dean Reilly stood up and walked across the rostrum to whisper in President Bieber's ear.

"Perhaps you are reluctant to come forward now," he resumed, "so I will delay my decision for another hour so someone can see me in private. We will all meet back here in the auditorium." There was another dramatic pause, then he continued, "the person that did this should know, we have some strong suspicions. It will be better for all, and that individual, if they come forward."

I was sure they were on to me. I realized all they had to do was see who signed out for walks yesterday. It was a solemn bunch of kids that filed back into the building an hour later with barely a murmur.

"I have been very patient with you. This is your last chance. I find it unbelievable that the person responsible is going to let everyone suffer for his or her stupidity. Not one student has come forward."

I was feeling truly awful. I didn't want to have the whole school punished. I was getting fidgety. It was an appropriate moment for my newfound Christian rectitude to rise to the occasion, but a little red creature on my Pat Knupp shoulder whispered, "Forget that old wind-bag. Wait and see what he does. You can always tell on yourself then." I waited.

"That's it. You leave me no choice." Mr. Beiber continued. "I must punish the whole school because of one individual." Another long pause. He turned to confer with Dean Reilly and Pastor Milner.

"As your Principal, I must say how disappointed I am in all of you. You will all now have to pay the price for that one student's actions. I regret to tell you that the marching social for this evening behind the girl's dorm is canceled."

There was a stunned silence, then both boys and girls leapt uncontrollably to their feet in an explosive roar of ear-shattering joy.

Ya jus' never know where the precious good times 're gonna' come from, but when they do jus' lie back, luxuriate, and know you must have done somthin' right for a change.

9

OH SHENANDOAH, I HEAR YA CALLIN'

My life as a yoyo was now in full swing.

The "Whiffenpoof" song was one of those classics for male choral groups, so popular in academia in the 1950s—thank you Yale University. You could not possibly be such a group and not have it in your repertoire. And indeed, we did sing the "Whiffenpoof" song in the newly formed male *a cappella* chorus. A slightly risqué departure from hymns, I admit, but one inconsistency I welcomed as a gasp of fresh, as opposed to recycled air.

Obviously, I was still having difficulty switching from anti-Adventist to being a baptized member of the church. Actually, being baptized hadn't simplified my life. Well, it got my father off my back, but being a baptized member of the church actually added a solution fraught with defects. The defects had to do with cleaning up my sin-laden soul now that God, via the church, had added me to his watch list.

There was a distinct possibility that it might relate to something my Uncle Phil had pointed out to me at the age of nine. It concerned the behavior of corporations, politicians, and much of humanity, but mostly the first two, in his opinion. And, truth be known, himself as well.

"They tended to solve an existing problem," he said, "by creating a new one, typically for someone else." It was a bit of a stretch, but what I had done was solve the problem of Milner and my father by holding my nose and getting baptized. But when I came up for air and took a look around, I realized the only thing I'd accomplished was to add a slurry of guilt to my meaty stew of anger. The problem had grown! It went from being out there, focused on the enemy, to being inside, focused on me. Here I was at the age of fourteen, falling right into step with everything my Uncle warned me about, but worse. This solution created a problem for me, not someone else. Then I did what everyone else does when confronted with a lame solution of their own making: I changed the subject.

Music became my clever diversion, "Whiffenpoof" or otherwise, that helped to hold my gulag-world, my father, and a portion of me at bay. And if a little was good, a lot would be better. The school choir was first, then the "Whiffenpoof" song, and when out of the blue, I was asked to be first tenor in the school quartet, I agreed. And I put my whole heart and being into it. It was the perfect setup for me. Because when I sang, nothing else existed but that space within my mind and heart, freeing me for a time from the moldering walls of my constricted life.

But nothing is perfect. Tragically, from my teenage perspective, the music actually brought me a modicum of tolerance and possibly even value in the eyes of the gatekeepers. The last thing I wanted from the likes of Pastor Milner and company was to be of value. Unfortunately, I now fit in.

I asked myself, was it a reasonable trade-off, fitting in? I hated myself for being so two-faced. Not that subverting the world of the adults was anything I hadn't tried before, which is the duty of every teenager with a modicum of spunk, but, and it was a big 'but', maybe the only 'but', I was baptized.

I hadn't planned on guilt. In my daily life since total immersion, I had quickly figured out how to cruise along on autopilot. I became easy with my guilt. It wasn't the real thing, Just some vague, nagging irritation that I kept locked away in a mental compartment. It's not that I took the baptism plunge lightly. Quite the opposite. I was now a true striving-to-be-a-better-member-of-the-church person. But I hadn't bargained on feeling guilt over everything for life, which is where things were headed. This being "accepted" as a baptized member was pressing hard against me. It was an insurmountable dilemma, a conflict between the church and me, the old guilt-free me and the new guilt-burdened me, even worse, my mounting guilt built up with God for my persistent pissy attitude. Of course, at the time, all this madness wasn't that precisely understood by me, but the waxing and waning feelings of guilt were. So, to rebalance myself against fitting in, I looked for something internally grounding, like the thought of poking a pointy stick in Milner's eye. Not much of a rebellion. Just a bit of diversion.

Actually, buried deep inside was the repressed need for a huge cathartic gotcha. One that would require intense focus, dedication, and strategic timing if it was to be a first-class-excellent-Milner-gotcha.

But Pastor Milner was behaving more prudently in his responses to me these days. After all, he was the winner in our struggle for my eternal soul. Irritating.

I didn't trust him.

Instead, I continued to mince around the Pastor. Couldn't afford to push it too far. After all, things were going better for me, and besides, he was my main safety relief valve in waiting on campus.

I didn't know if I was just a hard case or a typical teenager at odds with all things adult or in an arm wrestling struggle with myself? In fact, it was all of that.

Unfortunately, I didn't resolve any of it. I was, after all, only fourteen and because going for walks had none of that conflicted yes-I-will and no-I-won't about it. From the very first week of my freshman year, I understood that if I truly wanted to clear the static electricity from my brain, I needed to go for long walks, always best by myself. And it was the culprit of static electricity that not only survived my baptism intact but had actually increased. Being by myself allowed me to just be myself, to eliminate the self-chastising buzz in my ears.

Sundays were the best day for these mini time-out walks, the only day with nothing required of anyone other than morning and evening vespers.

I had been going on longer and longer free-ranging rambles since my return south to Virginia from a visit home. I had even kept my walks to the two designated directions set out by the school to keep boys and girls separated. There were also the occasional trips permitted into the village of New Market with not much there to do but buy toothpaste, visit the barbershop and eat some fried chicken (at the moment, and it was moment to moment) I was, on that particular afternoon, a confirmed Seventh Day Adventist vegetarian.

While walking about the village, I looked up and saw the Massanutten mountains a few miles to the east. They were only an hour's walk at most from the school. Though not in one of the permitted directions, I thought, so what: they need to be explored.

Just before Sunday breakfast I talked to the school cook and asked if she would make up a bag lunch for me. It would extend the comfort and range of my walk. The cook agreed.

After breakfast, I picked up lunch and left for the day. I couldn't follow the road to town, which would have been the most direct route. Someone might stop me. Instead, I signed out for a walk up the hill behind the barns. When I reached the top of the hill, I turned right through the woods, after which I continued through fields until I reached the village. Other than crossing Route Eleven, I choose to stay off any roads. Another few miles of fields brought me to the foot of the mountain ridge, well away from houses or people. I hadn't given this excursion much thought other than reaching my goal, which had not taken that long. I had many more hours remaining. The sun was warm, the adventure waiting, so into the woods and up the hillside I went. I didn't bother looking for a trail. My on-the-spot decision was to get to the top and back in the time I had. Looking for a trail might eat up too much time. I was hopeful that I'd find a clearing and get a grand view. Up and up I went in a straight line. Judging by the sun's location, I was doing quite well, but then the woods became too dense, the ground too strewn with debris, and the slope too steep to care about anything but climbing. In the way that hard work takes everything you have to offer, the climb consumed all of my concentration, and I lost all sense of time. The sole purpose of my effort became the next step. At times, the way was so steep it became more of a scramble than a hike. I stopped, more from exhaustion than hunger, against some rocks to eat my lunch. When I finished, I got up and found my rocky backrest was nearly a cliff that spread out and up forever, too much to find a way around. So up I went with the grade so steep it put my face only inches from the ground at times. The climb seemed interminable. This day had disintegrated into a boring chore. And then the slope ended abruptly, transitioning into a flat grassy area. More than surprised, it took a moment for this strangely tamed plot of grass to register after the wildness of the climb, when I realized not more than a few yards away, a large sliding doorway stood open in the side of a small barn.

What was it doing there on the side of the mountain in the middle of the forest? What should I do? Should I go in? The day had been hot, the effort extreme, and I was sweating profusely. A rest in a cool shaded place would be perfect. If I was discrete, quiet, maybe no one would notice me. The whole time I had been easing myself forward until I finally found myself inside the barn, where I sagged to the hay-covered floor to take a rest. It was cool and dark. At the opposite end of the barn was another large open doorway through which searing white sunlight was etching a rectangle into the straw strewn floor, making what lay beyond indistinct. Dust motes and lazing flies filled the air above the bleached rectangle. I looked away, waiting for my eyes to readjust to the dim interior. The barn felt old and tired. There were a couple of empty wooden stalls for large animals on the left, and on the right a walled-in area with a hayloft above. And then I saw what could only be a gigantic bearskin, hanging spread eagle on the wall to my right. I walked over to it. Only the head and front legs were close enough for me to reach. The rest was stretched far above my head, nailed to the wall. I had never seen a bear before, in or out of its skin.

I reached out to stroke the black fur paw, then let my fingers slide down along the hard lethal four-inch claws to feel their strength and sharpness. There seemed to be a thin, pale, yellow-orange edge around the pitch-blackness of the form, as it contrasted against the tan-ish color of the wood so that the whole skin seemed to float free of the wall.

I'd no understanding about what followed, but I felt a strange tightness, more like a tingling, beginning under my scalp and radiating to the back of my skull, filling my ears with a barely audible ringing as that subtle current filled my gut with a primal premonition.

I stepped back from that flattened bear volume to get a better view and wondered where North Jersey was? Bewildered, I turned and walked toward the sunlit doorway and was stopped by the crystal brightness that dimmed my view and made me wonder if what I saw was real.

A lush grass strip, the width of the door continued straight out from the barn to an inky forest wall where it ended a fair distance away. A cloudless cerulean sky made everything below seem dense and deeply colored against the acidic blue above: the oxblood earth, gray-blue rocks, a black, black tree stump, and a solitary shirtless man, weathered to the color of the earth, was sitting on that stump on the edge of the grass verge facing downhill. Behind him, on my left, a steep slope led up to a rude log cabin with a shed-roofed porch across the front, utilitarian at most in the best of times, now neglected but still in use. Nothing extraneous was about, no trash or tools, just firewood stacked under the porch roof. In front of the house was a terraced vegetable garden dormant in anticipation of the upcoming winter. The final terrace ended at a low fieldstone wall against the narrow grass strip.

The man on the stump sat sideways to me, maybe fifty feet off, working away on a second even larger black bearskin, scraping away at the flesh side, removing final bits of meat, I thought.

He seemed unaware of me. I had been cautious, moved slowly, even before I knew anyone was there. An overwhelming need to be respectful—even reverential—had swept over me the moment I raised my head above the edge of the steep climb. Its out-of-placeness made it seem possessed of a presence and mystery, as powerful as anything I'd ever experienced, and this frightened me too. Maybe it wasn't real, or I wasn't there? Maybe if I moved my hand too quickly or thoughtlessly inched a foot forward, everything would come undone. I looked for loose pebbles, even fallen autumn leaves that could sound an alert if I left the protection of the barn. If only I could float over the ground. I couldn't go forward, wouldn't go backward. But I needed to move. If I do and if this is real, what will he do, the man on the stump? He'd jump up, come after me? Or someone at the cabin would call out. Nothing happened. I walked toward the man. He didn't look up. Never changed his pace, just kept working, holding down the pelt with his right foot, while pulling against it with his left hand and with his right arm, made long powerful upward strokes with a broad knife, scraping the skin clean of meaty bits. I was now standing slightly behind him on his right. He was dressed just as you'd imagine, as an Appalachian man, like the farm boy in my imagination, all ragged and worn. Below him was a pasture with a lone milk cow. It all existed within a small forest clearing. When I had left the protection of the dark barn, I carefully made my way toward him by staying slightly uphill to avoid his peripheral vision, stopping cautiously behind him. But I couldn't see him working from that position, so pushing my luck, I moved closer, slightly off to his left within a few feet. There was no reaction. I was sure he knew

I was there. What now? I said to myself. The man never paused in his concentration to keep his knife at the best angle for slowly scraping the skin with long rhythmic strokes.

Barely over a whisper, I said, "Where am I?" and waited. I had never seen a bearskin before, nor such a man, nor such a farm, or even imagined any place like this outside the cover of a fairytale book. In reality, I wasn't asking where I was. I was asking if this place was real.

He didn't respond.

Well, of course, he didn't respond. None of this is real, was what went through my head again. Don't be stupid. Of course, he's real. You're standing here. Your eyes are open. You can feel the breeze. Just talk louder.

"Where am I, sir?"

He said nothing—felt no need to. Just continued to work. I knew I was unwanted. I stepped closer to watch the skill of his hands perform something I knew nothing about. It mesmerized me. That tingling feeling that began back in the barn became luscious. I didn't want to talk or move for fear this moment, this place, and his being, his methodical ancient skill, would evaporate.

And then the lusciousness became an instant rush of panic; I realized even more so this time how horribly out of place I was, like a fly in a glass of milk.

I glanced at the lowering sun. How had it gotten to be so late?

"I'm lost," I tried again, thinking that being lost might bring him 'round. It seemed as though I had stumbled through an unguarded spot in his invisible barrier where the air beyond the barrier was sweeter, the colors stronger, the sunlight cleaner, and everything just as perfect and complete as it should be, and I had no idea that this discovery was the reason for my walk. I don't know what really happened that day or the perfection of this memory. I do know something happened and that I felt something I've never felt again.

I have asked myself many times when that memory bubbles up, *Did that really happen?*

Oh yes, it did.

The way it felt?

Yes.

But why?

I've no idea. But someday I might.

He never looked up, he just kept working. I was now standing next to him hoping for an answer to my question. It seemed a eternity but then, without looking up, without slowing the rhythm of his work, he said, "Thou art of scant use to thyself." Then he pointed down the slope where I thought I could just make out a narrow opening in the woods. The path he stabbed at with his knife led me on a long downward trail that ended abruptly on the side of the mountain in the forest, not at a road, for no road led to his farm. From there on, I bushwhacked until I came out near the town of New Market. Too tired to care any longer if I would be seen, I walked back along the paved road till I reached the school, too late for evening vespers.

As I entered my room, *I thought, I'll certainly be punished for missing evening vespers.* What an amusing way to finish such a perfect, perfect day. Fledgling steps toward understanding the absurdity of life. I was growing up—or sideways.

I planned to return as soon as possible. Next Sunday. I even started out several times over several weeks, but something seemed to interfere too late in the day: a bad night's sleep, the walk too difficult, mostly silly things. It didn't matter. Certainly, a hundred-year wait didn't seem reasonable. *Maybe the same day next year, just in case?* Next year never came.

It was one of the most moving events of my childhood, revealing the nature of living out of touch with reality. Not the mountain man's—mine, ours. I have determined that the screwy nature and strange juxtaposition of events at that time were the doings, possibly, of my guardian angel or more likely, the three Greek fates, making capricious decisions for my future. They just neglected to inform me outright. Instead, they humorously chose to sprinkle clues along my rabbit-run life for me to follow or trip over, depending upon their mood.

What was I to make of this experience? It had a profound effect on me at the moment and even more so down through the years as I grew to understand why that day was such a profound experience. Those few words, "Thou art of scant use to thyself," have served me more effectively throughout my life than all the bribery, cajoling and badgering of my father, the school, church, my uncle... For I took it to mean everything is ultimately of your own doing, so don't do stupid things. The implication of, "Thou art of scant use to thyself," I realized was, "Unto thine own self be true."

What an unending joyful, painful task that has proved to be.

10

THE GET AWAY

Despite the overbearing malevolent environment we found ourselves in, my roommate and I managed to find ways to escape by being typical wacko teenage boys as an act of survival, only to have all of our efforts come to naught.

My first roommate, a religious zealot, fascinated me the same way a geek I once saw in a pit at a carnival did, by biting off the heads of live chickens. He and I didn't last. I got along fine with Bart and Charlie. Then there was that peculiarity of Arthur's. He was gay. That was how I thought of it then. Even so, I still did like him. Herbie was my last and longest roommate. We were together for more than a year and had what I thought of at the time as a workable friendship: dependable, respectful, and in many ways, a tacit understanding of the micro-world surrounding us.

We often went on walks together. None of those hell-bent affairs from my junior year. Just nice, normal walks: a cave once in a while, an easy scramble up a cliff, no potential for bodily harm unless you consider teenage impulsiveness innately dangerous. We didn't.

We were out on a stroll one Sunday afternoon along the north/south railroad tracks on the other side of the Shenandoah River. It's always hard to walk on tracks. The cross ties aren't spaced quite right for comfort. They're too close together for a normal stride. It was better for Herbie's longer legs to span every other cross tie, but not mine. I was up on the rail doing a passable balancing act, actually keeping up with Herb's leisurely pace. We were discussing the dreariness of classwork, which was beginning to spill over into a kind of feeling-sorry-for-ourselves gossipy way.

"There's a train comin,'" I announced. I could feel it through my shoes. I got down, turned, and looked back. I could see about a half-mile down the line where the tracks bent off to the left. The train wasn't in sight. Herbie didn't respond. That is, he didn't speak; instead he pulled a handful of quarters out of his pocket. I knew immediately what he was up to. We'd had this conversation before.

"Don't you do it," I said.

"Do what?" He had a big smirk on his face.

"You know. It might just work."

It was one of those teen legends—if you put a stack of five quarters on the rail, it would tip a train over.

"I don't believe that." Herb was straining to look serious.

"Is that why you wanted to come this way?"

"Oh no. I jus' thought of it."

"And you jus' happin' ta have a bunch of quarters with you...?"

We were both standing next to the tracks now. He reached down and placed the five coins in a perfect stack on the rail.

"You wanna go ta jail for murder? It'll kill your mother." I knew that sounded lame.

He was doing his best to stifle a laugh. "My mother! My mother? Is that your best..? My Mommy won't like it?"

• • •

Herbie's mother, Peg, was an RN and a member of the Adventist Church. At some point during his childhood, his mother had been baptized. His father never. Unlike my family, his parents were able to accommodate their differences. Yet there was a parallel aspect to both our lives; neither of us was born into the Adventist church. Most of the students at the school were "lifers." This was a new realization for me, and I would never have understood that if we hadn't been roommates. It wasn't based on anything either one of us had said. Herb seemed more natural to me, and also relaxed, as was I, about the prophetic soon-to-occur end-of-the-world and other Adventist things like not eating meat, especially Virginia ham, out of this world delicious and made right there in New Market. That made it most unlikely that either of us would be "saved." Herbie and I had had a life before "the church."

I thought of us as aliens in a foreign principality, pretending all was normal even though, in any context, we were still insanely impulsive teenagers. Not overtly rebellious, which was Herbie's natural state, no one singled us out, not often anyway, but admittedly, we spoke the Adventist language with a noticeable accent. Mine was often tinged with the sinful smell of coffee. Well, it was near impossible to stop drinking the stuff since I started at the age of three. Coffee-milk is what my Dutch family called it.

In general, I was more stressed than Herb about being stranded in that foreign village. Though we never expended much energy on the subject, I sensed there was an underlying understanding that we were trapped at that school and were trying to make the best of things. He just wasn't interested in talking about our mutual disquiet. That's what it was, for me at that moment, repressed disquiet. I repressed; Herb ignored.

All in all, I felt fortunate to have him as a roommate. We were not just schoolmates thrown together by chance. I actually liked him. We became friends. He was solid, even-tempered, and we had fun together, which helped me rise above my darkest introspections. And that was more than enough, far more than any other roommate. We trusted each other. Though I liked Charlie, he and I seemed to always go our separate ways. Together Herb and I could be just two teenage boys, able to behave the way teenage boys behave anywhere, doing creative, dumb, impulsive things on a regular basis. Impulsive behavior was not new to me. The difference now, I had a dependable fellow conspirator to share those wacky moments with.

I put my ear to the track. "It's almost here, Herbie. What are ya gonna' do?"

He balanced the stack of quarters on the rail.

I waited for a response then dove for the quarters. We had stopped on the side of the single track. He reached down and grabbed my foot, and pulled me back. He fell over on top of me, and we rolled down the bank a few yards. Then he got up and went to restack the coins. The train was now in sight. I got up to stop him. We were both now within inches of the stacked coins. Several hundred feet wouldn't have been enough distance to be safe. What if he was right? What if the train derailed? I went after the coins again. There wasn't time to get to safety.

It was a large freight train headed north. "Do you want to kill somebody?" The train was nearly upon us. He started throwing rocks at me to distract me. He grabbed my foot again and pulled me a few feet toward the bank. I couldn't look away. It was too late. The engine came thundering at full speed. There was a loud snapping sound, and I saw the front wheel of the diesel engine leap into the air and watched as the whole hulking mass twisted sideways off the track. There was a horrific screeching metal sound, things flew through the air, all around…

"All right, chicken," he yelled as the freight cars rumbled past, inches away. "You can open your eyes now."

"What happened?" which was silly since I was obviously still alive. I turned my head to watch the tail end of the train disappearing to the north.

"Nothing. The quarters fell off the track just before the train got here." He went to pick up his money. "Vibration, I guess."

"Hey, look." He held up one paper-thin crushed quarter. "Pretty neat, huh?"

"Yeah, look how the head is all stretched out. Ya know Herb, I bet if you tape the coins to the track, it would work."

I'm Not Here

With a smirky glint in his eye, Herb said, "Why don't we come back tomorrow with tape, then you'll really have something to tell my mommy." We both doubled over laughing.

We were both good at problem-solving. We just weren't good at picking the right problems. He was the one who helped me put the ten brown bats in my flashlight, so I could bring them back to school and let them go in the auditorium during Friday night church. Now that was a class A solution to a problem we weren't even thinking about. We were a team.

Cassy Teal, a good old southern boy, southern first, Adventist second, used to go on walks with us once in a while. I really liked Cassy. He had a zany personality and was more interested in having fun then almost anything having to do with remembering the rules. Cassy had been to town and unbeknownst to us bought some two-inch firecrackers. Being able to buy fireworks as a teenager was beyond my comprehension, though I saw billboard ads everywhere. That is until Cassy. We were on a walk. Cassy was about ten paces ahead of us. He lit a firecracker, an ashcan actually, the fuse comes out of the side, not the end, they make a louder noise, and he dropped it on the ground. Just as we came even with that spot, the cracker went off. Like a gunshot. Scared us silly. We chased him, but he got away. Of course, we saw him back at school, but that was different. We were all trapped. It would have been unfair to get even then, and we needed to get even. But we waited, for a long time, until getting even seemed like a thing forgotten, didn't count anymore.

A few weeks later, all three of us were on a walk again. Herb and I had carefully planned for the walk to pass through a pasture filled with fresh cow pies. My job was to go ahead and plant a firecracker. Herb's was to start a disagreement about which baseball team was the best, a topic I was ill-prepared to handle since I shared the Southern penchant to hate the Yankees. In the South, the Yankees were the team detestable, vile, revolting, abhorrent, loathsome. My team, the Brooklyn Dodgers, weren't quintessentially Northern enough to get a rouse out of sassy

Cassy. Of course, Herb was arguing that the Yankees were the best, as he often explained to me, creating my only bone of contention with him. In fact, in the 1950s, the Yankees seemed invisible. And they really were. Knowing that this was like waving a red flag in front of any good southern boy was the perfect ploy for setting Cassy up for the kill. And it worked, just as we expected. At the last second, Herbie jumped safely away as Cassy got splattered with wet, sticky cow manure. There's nothing sweeter than teenage revenge except the memory of it. Cassy was splattered with brown globs, head to foot. The two of us laughed so hard we fell down. An excellent plan masterfully executed, except the cow-goo-boy immediately got even with us by cleaning the worst off himself while hovering over us. We all wound up rolling around on the ground laughing.

At some point in life, you learn that the end of one thing is never an end but the start of something else, usually unanticipated. That's why many people turn to religion, I speculated, to rein things in, make them predictable. For Herbie and I, this entire cow pie event fomented a plethora of teenage creativity completely unheard of in the annals of Shenandoah Valley Academy history, at least in our imaginations.

We made a Zip gun. Aah, yes! My moment of submissive timidity had passed. My old sneaky self had re-emerged. Herbie's too. Neither of us knew anything about the history of Zip guns being the plague of city life at the time. We invented it out of hand as an original creation. One of us, I don't recall which, came up with the idea of making that firecracker gun. It consisted of a six-inch piece of three-quarter-inch pipe, a pipe cap with a hole drilled in it. How we accomplished that, I've no idea. There was no handle, no trigger, just an exposed fuse to be lit with one hand while the other held the pipe aimed in the general direction of something easy, like the side of a barn.

Until three weeks before, it never occurred to Herb or me to buy fireworks. Herb had snuck into Cassy's room and stole one for our moment of retribution. Now we dreamed and schemed of doing nothing else but making this Zip gun. In order to do this, we had to do three things that were not a part of the school's plan for our salvation: 1) We had to go into town on the wrong day of the month, we just couldn't wait, 2) we had to sign out for a walk and then go in the wrong direction, and 3) very, very wrong—we had to buy fireworks. I got that job by being the one with the least common sense.

The isolated store was on the north end of the New Market village on route eleven across from an open field.

"I'd like a two-incher, please."

"Can't do it."

"You can't?" I figured I was too young. "I'm really sixteen. That's okay, isn't it?"

"Yup."

"You need proof?"

"Nope."

The store wasn't large. The walls were covered with shelves floor to ceiling and were filled with enough stock to wipe the town off the planet.

"I saw y'all sneakin' down the hill over yonder," he finally continued. "Must be from that school."

I knew he meant SVA. "You mean the Academy?" I said in a weak moment of defensive pride, which left me with a feeling of self-betrayal. "That why you can't sell me fireworks?" Of course the school had put the word out about selling to the lambs of the church.

"No. Y'all gotta buy a whole box."

"Oh, okay! All right! How much?" It was around five dollars, a lot of money. But there were a whole lotta two-inchers in the box.

Later that same afternoon, back at the Academy, Herb and I headed out to put our invention to the test. The only convenient side of a barn to shoot at was the school's barn, within sight of the dorms. We weren't that impulsive. So, we headed out to the lower pasture near the river to find some cows with our untried gun, a large ammo collection of hard rose hips, selected for humane consideration more for ourselves than the cows, and proceeded to pepper every critter's rump in sight. Word was that among the dairy workers at breakfast the next morning, no one could figure out why the cows didn't milk well that day. Herb and I rushed back to our room for a private moment of ecstatic teen jubilation, which was quickly followed by, "What the hell were we thinking."

That afternoon we threw the pipe in the river, the remaining firecrackers too.

Things didn't always work out. We jimmied a window in a vacant house located on the far side of the river about two miles from the school. We did a tour of the first floor and started on the second when we heard a man yelling for us to get out of the house. He was on the front porch fumbling with his keys, trying to unlock the door when we crashed down the stairs within inches of the door, rounded the newel post, raced to the rear of the house, jumped out the window just ahead of the grasping hands of the man and ran off into the woods. That was a close call, but we got away clean. When we got back to school an hour later, Dean Reilly was waiting for us on the front porch.

"Could I trouble you boys for a minute before you get cleaned up for dinner?" Dean Reilly was a master at misdirection.

We followed him into his office, where a man was having a cup of tea. "Those are the boys," he said, getting to his feet. And then he lied and said we broke the front door glass and that he wanted payment. We had done nothing to damage the house, nor would we have, being two good Christian house-breakers. The window was cracked down the middle when we first got there. We had tried the door to see if it was open. After the man left, we heatedly explained this to the Dean—that the man was a liar, to no avail.

"You entered the house illegally," the Dean explained. "He could have you boys arrested for breaking and entering."

I'm Not Here

That was startling information for our teenage minds to grasp. But we recovered quickly. There was no breaking involved, we pointed out, only entering. Didn't matter. We had to pay the deceitful, opportunistic creep sixteen dollars for a window that was already broken, and we had to do it by walking to his house telling him we were sorry—SORRY—while putting the money in his hand, another one of Dean Reilly's creative punishments. It took every bit of money we had between us and we were grounded for two weeks; it was a close second to going to jail.

. . .

Immediately after my illegal house entering, sans break in, I resorted to a contrived malaise, ho-humming my way through every day, filling it up with teeth brushing, daydreaming, floor polishing, better than anyone ever had, reading sinful Jules Verne books by flashlight. My Grandparents had given me a beautiful, color-illustrated, four-book set of his best-known works for my eighth birthday: Twenty Thousand Leagues Under the Sea, Around the World in Eighty Days, Journey to the Center of the Earth, The Mysterious Island. They were the size of coffee table books, and they were saving my life from abject disinterest now that I had returned to a low profile existence. In addition to loving the books for what they were, they were the only tangible link to my childhood, to my Grandparents and the vanished mother of that childhood who often read to me from these books before they were deemed Satanic.

One day, in a minuscule act of brazenness, I moved the evil novels I had stored safely out of sight in a box under my bed to the desk I shared with Herbie. He never showed any interest in them other than looking at the pictures. Nor did anyone else.

And then something changed. Out of some dark recess of my mind, a squeaky clean, though obsessed version of me emerged, plopped down on top of the already muted me, and convinced me to refrain from tipping over trains, drinking coffee, breaking

113

into houses, seasoning people with cow doo doo, and most of all, to not shoot cow derrieres with rose hips ever again. That I should be concerned about the kind of person I was becoming.

This came on me suddenly. One day as I was guilty of lusting after a juicy bacon hamburger or trips to the movies, I found a profound impulsive teenager-need to be abstemious of all earthly desires. It must have been that classic confused adolescent questioning of 'who am I'? What should I do with my life, other than think about my budding libido, listen to Rock 'n' Roll on my illegal radio, secretly read Jules Verne, and go on misadventures with Herbie? It was the great yawning canyon of an uncertain eternity that I sensed was tripping toward me. This sort of thing had happened to me before, and it was doing it again, this swing from nary-a-care-in-the-world-boredom to feeling guilty, this time guilty enough to act on it.

This sincere personal effort to salvage my soul lasted from the day I paid the man for the broken window until the day Herbie came running toward me frantically calling my name. A week or so anyway.

"Jerry... Jerry something terrible..." I took a deep breath. *Oh! Thank God, errr, rather, Thank Goodness, a distraction, something real.*

It was about three in the afternoon. I had just finished work and was on my way back to the dorm to get cleaned up. He didn't stop to tell me what it was. Instead, he turned and ran toward the dorm, waving for me to follow. We flew through the front door, past boys that were drifting through their afternoon. On up the stairs two at a time, round the turn at the top, down the hall to crash through our door.

The room was trashed: drawer contents dumped out, mattresses on the floor, the bedding torn apart. Our clothes had been dragged from the closet and ripped apart. My Jules Verne books lay on the desk with pages slashed, torn from their covers.

I didn't know what to do or say. We stood there in the ruin for several minutes, staring at the room and each other.

"I'm gonna' get the dean."

"No point. He won't do anything," Herb said.

"Why not?"

"No one will rat out the boys that did this. We're just Yankees. They hate us. We're not good enough."

"What do you mean, we're not good enough?"

"We're jus' not."

"When did you find this Herb?"

"A few minutes before I saw you."

It suddenly struck me. He was right. "What can we do?" All the past four years in that school came flooding over me in a wave of anger and depression. What good had it done to try to fit in, to make them think I was a real believer?

"I'm getting out of here, Herb added. "I don't want to be anyplace where people don't want me."

"What are you talkin' about?"

"I'm gonna' leave here first thing in the morning. Why don't you come with me?"

"Where will you go? How will you get there? Do you have any money?"

"Home! I'll hitchhike like you do. Please come with me. You know the way to go."

My mind went blank.

"They did this to both of us."

"It's so confusing, Herb."

Despite all my effort to fit in, no matter what, way down inside, I knew I still hated being in that school. But going home? To something that caused all my problems?

"Our parents will kill us," I cautioned.

"Not when they learn what happened. My father will be so angry at this place. I'll bet your father will be too, Jerry."

No, he wouldn't. I knew he wouldn't. I could see him. He'd pull his lips into a tight thin line. His eyes, too, would become slits. He'd take a deep breath and hold it, and when he let it out, the interrogation would begin that would grind me down. My only hope, if I went home, was my mother. Maybe the 'old' mother that resisted him in the past would re-emerge to help me.

"All right," was all I could manage to say. I was trapped between two ugly worlds. There was no one I could turn to. No other place to be. It wasn't a good decision, but the pain of staying was far worse at that moment than the pain of facing what I knew was waiting for me at home.

"All right? You'll go?"

"I'll go." It was two months before my graduation.

We didn't tell anyone. We did what we always did: went to dinner, Friday night church service, then back to our room to sleep after we straightened it up a bit. The next morning, we packed a few things and crept out of the dorm at first light. We walked to town and started hitchhiking. We got a ride up into the Blue Ridge Mountains within a few minutes as far as Luray. And then nothing; for five hours we stood in the village of Luray.

Herbie had no idea what it meant to hitchhike three hundred fifty miles home. I knew that if we didn't get a ride soon, we would have to go back. It was a nine-hour drive straight through. It was nearly eleven. We had only covered a half-hour of that distance. I told Herbie what I realized. He wanted none of it. He was going on. I told him I'd wait another half hour, which was crazy. Even if we got a ride all the way home, we wouldn't get there until around eight o'clock at night.

A short time later, we got a ride to D.C. Not great, but better than being stuck in Luray. D.C. was a hard place to get a ride. We could get stranded there.

The only money between us was the little I had. It wasn't enough to get back or go home if we couldn't get a ride. I had a bad feeling. It was much harder to get rides with two of us, and we were now too far from school to return easily. So on we went. I don't recall how we covered the rest of the distance. I do remember finishing the final leg by bus from Newark. There was just enough money for that. I walked in the door close to ten at night.

My parents were sleeping. But my mother heard me come in. She got up. She placed a finger across her pursed lips to shush me.

I whispered, "I can't take it anymore."

"Tomorrow," she said. Then she helped me open the hide-a-bed in the front of the trailer. While I got undressed, she made me a peanut butter sandwich, and a glass of milk then went back to bed.

When I woke early the next morning, my parents were sitting at the table eating breakfast, dressed for church.

"Get ready for church," said my father. "We'll talk later. There's no time now." His face said what his words did not.

We left for church. As soon as I could, I slipped out and went to the diner for a cup of coffee. Why not? My parents were standing outside the church talking to the minister when I got back.

"Where were you?"

"I went for a walk."

My mother looked at my father nervously. My father looked at the minister nervously, and the minister looked at me and smiled weakly.

"Let's get in the car."

It was a short ride back home that couldn't last long enough for me, but when we got there, I didn't care any longer.

The angry word-sounds began. I didn't need to listen. It was like the price of admission to a terrible movie. I waited for the angry sounds to end, but they outlasted me.

"You're going back."

"What about my room and things?"

"I called the school and talked to Dean Reilly. They'll let you come back so you can graduate."

"What about going—"

"It's too late to go anywhere else. I was on the phone for a long time. You're going back. I'm driving you all the way there tomorrow."

"What about all my wrecked stuff?"

"They think you did it."

"We did not! They tore up my books, all my clothes. I've got nothin' to wear."

"Those un-Godly books were not allowed. It's better that they're gone. We'll send you some clothes."

We left at midnight. Got to the school just before nine in the morning. A half-hour later, my parents started the return trip after meeting with Dean Reilly. They never went upstairs to see what had happened. Herbie got back that afternoon. His parents dropped him off.

"They think we trashed our own room. Why would we do that?"

"I know," said Herbie. "My mother told me. She said we're lucky they let us back in. Lucky! You feel lucky? I fucking don't."

It took me days to deal with my destroyed things. I had fallen in love with the memories they offered.

About seven years after graduation, Herbie called. I hadn't seen him since. He asked for my forgiveness. For what I wanted to know? He explained that he was the one that had destroyed all our things. Could I ever forgive him? I said forget it. We were just silly teenagers then. Besides, it was one of my favorite memories from all my years at that school. I asked why the sudden need to confess. He said he was returning to the Adventist Church and needed to take care of past misdeeds. "Well." I said. "Good luck with that one." And then I felt sadly alone.

11

Yeah, Right

As a child, I made up stories that altered situations I didn't like or understand. I called them "What-if" stories. In one such story, I incorporated the bomber Enola Gay (used to bomb Hiroshima) in an effort to thwart my father's intention to send me to a religious boarding high school. Four years earlier, that story took a bad turn with me being thrown out of the plane over the very school I was trying to avoid. Four years later, on the verge of graduation, and for good reason, I returned to my childhood remedy. The story begins.

The Enola Gay never made it to that airfield in Florida. Instead, it had circled the skies for four years over the Shenandoah Valley Academy.

I hadn't made up a story of any kind for a long time, that's if I didn't include lying. I mean a What-If-Story. And while I told myself the year before that I had given up such childish things, I was now, without admitting it, desperate. The last true one was four years ago when I was trying to not find myself at Shenandoah Valley Academy in New Market, Virginia. Now I was trying to escape the looming, even inevitable ambiguity of my life. In a few weeks, I'd be graduating. I wanted to go to college. Molly Schwartz, the barkeep next door to my childhood home, and my communist Uncle Phil, who lived upstairs, had drummed that idea firmly into my head along with my father, to a degree, but only if it was an Seventh Day Adventist school.

He was the only one willing to pay unless I would reconsider my uncle's offer to study art in Russia. Washington Missionary College was what my father had in mind, outside of D.C. It felt like an out-of-the-frying-pan-into-the-fire kind of idea. I had investigated other schools on my own. My GPA was too low. Only the Adventists would have me. But then they sort of had to since I was an Adventist. And though it had been an uphill struggle to become one, according to my father,(or downhill slide because I gave in to him) I felt a certain responsibility to that decision. Or, then again, maybe I was just pretending.

. . .

"Gallin, why are we still doin' this?" Rocky, the co-pilot, was speaking to the pilot. Everyone else called him Gale or Captain.

"You know why," said Casey, the bombardier.

"Yeah. Right. Tell me again. Maybe it'll make sense to me this time."

"Come on, Rocky. You know the reason why Captain is doing this," said the navigator, Terry.

"Because he has had second thoughts about throwin' the twerpy kid out before we got to West Virginia? Yeah, I know. It's been almost four years. Besides, who cares. That snot nose wouldn't even tell us his right name. "

Rocky was the bad-ass in the crew.

The Enola Gay had been flying low level reconnaissance over the Shenandoah area, looking for some evidence of where they threw me out of the plane. They had gotten as far as Georgia before Gale turned the plane around. He was also flying low for a second reason: to avoid radar detection.

. . .

One evening David walked up to me and said, "Why don't you and Charlie and I go for a walk tomorrow?" David and I,

I'm Not Here

David, from the same church back home, had little to do with each other during our four years at Shenandoah. Back home, we had planned to room together, but at the last moment, he backed out. We remained, if not friends, friendly, though distant. I found it peculiar that he should suggest we go on a walk together in the last few moments of the school year. It seemed out of place for David to suggest it, his personality being so restrained, remote, and during the suggested walk, very uncomfortable. The incongruity of his reawakened awareness of my existence intrigued me. I said yes out of curiosity. My old roommate Charlie also agreed to come along as well.

Besides, I was through with solitary walks, especially my solitary life. I had re-emerged out of the self-indulgent swamp of my mind for at least the last few weeks to be a member in good standing in this monastic teenage boot camp. If nothing else, I was, alas, that skilled chameleon. My basic strategy from childhood, even pre-Adventist, was to avoid standing out so I could go my own way. It had taken me nearly four years to assume the local coloration, but finally, after several false starts, I had achieved success: anonymity. But I was mistaken. My talent to fit in backfired. Somehow my artistic skills, nearly forgotten by myself, became desirable now that I fit in so well. Heaven knows how this notice occurred since any attention to aesthetic concerns in this visually myopic world was relegated to a stringent Victorian dress code, institutional pastel colors, and syrupy paintings of an Anglo-Saxon-looking Semitic Jesus. Over time, through numerous opportunities to observe the world, I have found that there's nothing like the evangelical (the world is about to end) Protestant mind to eviscerate one's aesthetic soul. Maybe it was due to the personalized repainting of my room, along with a large braided rug from home, heavy drapery, and soft table lamp lighting instead of institutional mint green walls, bare floors, a torn window shade, and a bare hundred-watt light bulb in the ceiling, found in most other rooms, that placed me beyond the pale. In a pinch, maybe it even made me the go-to-guy for artistic needs in the closing moments of the senior year. Or, it could have been my supreme ability at painting the boy's dorm entry windows. Whatever it was, I was asked to design the '56 class pennant, a device I personally found to be peculiar. And I also worked on the yearbook and helped decorate for the Senior Banquet. I did all three cheerfully and enjoyably. But it is the Banquet I remember most clearly, not for the most unforgettable decorative work that was done, but for the bizarreness of the event itself. In most other high schools, this event would be called a prom: the word prom indicating that everyone should be dressed formally in tuxedos and ball gowns, that there would be a formal sit down dinner at a local banquet hall, followed by dancing to a live band, after which couples would get into cars and head off to home parties or somewhere more intimately private until late in the morning. This was, in reality, meant to be a rite of passage into adult life.

At a Senior Banquet, we ate a faux meat entree with overcooked veggies from the cafeteria, and if I'm not mistaken, an approximation of Butterscotch pudding for dessert. This was then followed by an evening of the recurrent mechanical pattern marching to lovingly familiar recordings of John Phillip Susa band music, with the 36-inch rule of separation enforced, possibly relaxed somewhat. I think we were allowed to brush hands with the opposite sex. Producing new progeny for the church in the near future might have been considered in this pretended relaxation of standards.

The boys would be dressed in their dark Sabbath suits with a gardenia in their lapels, and the girls in long Antebellum gowns, sans significant décolletage, with orchid corsages on their left shoulders. After which, at the termination of festivities, each person walked back to their respective dorms by nine-thirty, in the certain knowledge that this was their rite of passage into a life that required repression of stimulating aesthetics, culinary excellence, expressive movement, and human sexuality if they cared to give the evening some thought, which I didn't at the time. I merely felt it was another strange aberration in a long line of them.

My return to the fold, artistic endeavors as well, was, in an unacknowledged way, a last-ditch effort to run out the school year. And I threw myself into it. And part of that return was going on that walk with David.

. . .

"You know, I'm only the lowly bombardier, but we've been doing this flying around rural Virginia now for three years, eight months, two weeks, four days and fourteen hours, and a bit more without a break or any success. It would've been easier to fly the twerp to Montana back then. I'm not getting any younger, Captain. We haven't seen any sign to let us know where we dumped him out. We need a new idea, or we need to quit."

"He's right Gallin," said Co-pilot Rocky. (Rocky, a man's man, had never gotten used to the fact that all of his fellow crew members had girls' names.) "What do you think, Terence?"

Terry, the navigator, a stand-behind-his-man kind of guy, looked at Rocky and Casey and said, "Let's give it one more try, for the great old guy runnin' this show. Ya know his heart's in the right place. That okay with you, Gale? One more time?"

Ignoring Terry for the moment, Gale said, "Oh, Casey! Casey, don't be so hard on yourself—a lowly bombardier. You're a vital, intelligent team player. And I value every word you utter." The Captain, with a display of sudden unexplained URGENCY looked away from everyone. He had to. He had inadvertently eased the plane down just below tree level.

"How 'bout you guys? Rocky? Casey?" prodded Terry.

"One more time," said Casey begrudgingly, "then we go home. Ya know Gale—my two kids are halfway through elementary school since you started this search. "

"Captain?"

Nothing.

"Gale?" Rocky said impatiently.

"I got it. I'm doin' it now. Our last run."

"JESUS H. CHRIST, WHAT THE HELL ARE YOU DOING, GALlIN? YOU TRYIN' TA TRIM HEDGES?" Rocky said.

"If this is our last darn run. I want it to be our best shot," said Gale.

"Hey. Look at that tree up ahead. It's got parachute shards in it," said Terry. "Looks like some kind of institution there. A school maybe?"

"You're right," Casey said. " It must be his school. The one he was tryin' so hard to avoid."

"How terrible for him," said Gale. "I feel awful."

"Oh, come on. What a f***ing lucky kid. He got out of grubby a**hole Paterson. It was Paterson, right guys? And got to spend four years in beautiful rural Virginia. Why are we even lookin' for the little f***er. There's only two weeks left in his last f***ing year, and you still wanna f***ing rescue him? He tried to hijack the plane for gosh sakes. With a stupid pee-poor cap pistol." Rocky could swear and curse with the best of them when the situation warranted it but chose to be considerate of Gale's delicate avoidance of such words. For reasons of persuasiveness.

"Well, Rocky, you make good sense, but it's the principle of the thing. I did him wrong, and we're gonna' make it up." The pilot was giving Rocky his best Air Force officer, power look.

"GOD DAMN IT, GALLIN! LOOK OUT FOR THAT COW."

. . .

I was sitting on the front steps of the dorm, with a big shitty grin on my face, waiting for David and Charlie, so we could start on our walk. The whole What-If story thing had only taken a few minutes to dream up while I was sitting there. It might have been four years since the last time, but I fell right back into the groove, though never had my past stories been so silly. I realized it but was helpless to stop my mind from going there. My first What-If story was at the age of eight. Back then, they all tended to involve serious role-playing.

But now, like a chain smoker hoping for the best, I said to myself, this must be my last one. It was time to grow up, but I needed to do this now. Just one more time.

I didn't hear David and Charlie walk out onto the porch behind me until David spoke. "Whatever are you snickering at out here all by yourself?"

"That you, David?" I asked.

"Are you asleep Jerry?"

"Na. Just thinkin.'"

His look showed incredulity at such possible mental activity.

Actually, my very last thought about growing up was trying to not think about growing up, but that was not possible with graduation and the rest of my life just around the corner. It was like the time Rufus stuck his head into my room and said, "Don't think of an elephant," then chuckled and ran off, like a hit-and-run driver.

"Where ya wanna go?" said Charlie.

"The permitted walk-direction is out back today," I said. I wanted to go to First Cliffs. It would probably be the last time, ever, that I would go there. Instead, I said, "You guys decide." If I was meant to go, it would happen.

Serendipity alive and well, David said, "Let's go toward First Cliffs. But down along the river."

We set off across the fields to the river, then turned to the right onto a dirt farm lane that petered out at the edge of a wooded area. The forest floor below the leaf canopy was uncluttered and quiet. We walked for a bit around a bend in the river. The cliff rose up on the right through the trees. David and Charlie were talking.

"You guys want to climb the cliff?" I had scaled this sheer stonewall many times over the past several years. I suddenly realized I needed to get to the place where I had soared above the lookout point with the red-tailed hawks.

On a previous walk two years earlier, I found myself at a stop at the place we called First Cliffs sitting in the midst of a carpet of mountain pinks looking out at the valley and the river below and the hawks circling overhead. A complete sense of peace and wellbeing came over me and I suddenly found I was high up in the sky soaring with the hawks. I was a hawk. And I looked down at my body sitting on the cliff's edge looking out at the valley.

I couldn't tell them that because of a tacit trust I felt existed between myself, that day, and the hawks. Besides I knew that neither they, nor anyone else in my life would ever believe I had left my body and became a hawk.

. . .

"That was too damn—ah, sorry Gallin—dang close. We need to do this a different way." Rocky was not only a badass potty mouth, he was the backup thinker in the crew after Gale, and right now, Gale didn't seem to be in his right mind.

"We need to get rid of this plane," The Rock said. "Get a small one. One that we could land in a field near that school."

. . .

"I don't feel at all like climbing," said David. "Do you want to, Charlie?"

"Umm. No, I don't think so. I'd rather go sit by the river. Jus' watch the river 'en the birds."

"Yes. Me too. Why do you want to climb?" said David. "Why don't you stay with Charlie and I?"

I wanted to go with them, and I didn't. Did he say, "and I"? Was that right?

"Well, I really feel like a climb." I said breezily, "So I'll see you guys later. Okay?"

"Will you be coming back down this way? Or will you get back to school from the top of the cliff? It seems a bit foolhardy to climb alone." David seemed genuinely concerned or logical. I wasn't sure how to read him.

"Yeah, okay. No, I do it all the time. I'll come back this way."

• • •

The crew looked at Captain Gale for a response. Even though he was busy pulling the four-engine plane up above the tree line, he could feel their eyes on him. He had heard Rocky's concern, which seemed to jolt his thoughts back on track. "Okay... I know where to get a Piper Cub."

• • •

I might be graduating in two weeks, but I wasn't looking forward to what was next. I had waited so long to get this whole thing over with. But after all these years of religious schooling, I was cut off from my past. I was now a church member in good standing if I or anyone else didn't look too closely, a convert on the surface, a covert cynic in my guts. A four-year wait to get this over with was only the beginning. Whatever was next, I feared, would only be a continuation.

I had lost interest in figuring out David's reasons for including me in this hike. I had an actual vibrational need centered right in my solar-plexus, to get to that place on top of that cliff, and I damn well knew why: to feel whole within myself, to fly away with the hawks and be rescued, even if for a short time.

As I walked through the trees to the base of the cliff, the litany for my What-If story came flooding back into my imagination. "Not now." I tried to explain to my imagination, "I've got something more serious to do."

• • •

The plane banked to the right and started north up the valley.
"Where ya takin' us, Gale?"
"To Arthur Godfrey's place."
"Arthur who?"
"Godfrey. Don't you know? He has a radio show in the mornings. Five days a week."
"Why there?"

. . .

As I moved unrushed toward the base of the cliff, I look up at the blue crazy-quilted sky through the broken forest canopy, trying not to think about this What-If story. But I sensed something was not quite right about it. Then I remembered. The story four years ago did the same thing. It took on a life of its own. I lost control of it. Instead of the Enola Gay being my means of escape from boarding school, it delivered me there. And I knew, absolutely knew, the guys up in that plane weren't coming to save me any more than they tried to help me the last time.

. . .

"Oh yeah. Now I remember," Casey said, looking thoughtfully up at the roof of the pilot's cabin, "Yeah, 'The Breakfast Club,' that show. It's live, and everybody gets up, Right? En' marches 'round the breakfast tables to music, singin' 'First call to breakfast, Everyone called to breakfast'. Er' somethin'."

"No, you dumb butt. That's the Don McNeill show. Everybody knows that." Terry said, anxious to get back to business. "What's Godfrey got to do with us anyway, Gale?"

Gale, a man unable to correctly prioritize the needs of life, a serious flaw for a pilot, let alone pilot of the historic Enola Gay, responded, "Godfrey's on late mornings, plays the ukulele... Real nice guy. Down-home folksy type. You got it, Casey? And by the

I'm Not Here

way. The name of Godfrey's show is, 'The Arthur Godfrey Time' not 'The Breakfast Club.' He then redeemed himself by nicely segueing into, "Godfrey has a place in the Blue Ridge Mountains. He's got a landing strip and a couple 'a small airplanes. I'm hopin' we can sort 'a borrow one."

"If we survive the landing, you mean." *Terry was perusing his charts just then and saw where Godfrey's place might be.* "Looks to me like the strip is about three hundred yards short followed by a sharp drop-off."

"Short? What...? Oh...! We've got a decent headwind. That'll help," *said Gale.* "I'll reverse the props too. That'll also slow us, and maybe I'll just have to belly flop 'er in as well. Between those three things, we ought 'a stop before that drop-off. Ya know, this old crate took off from the deck of an aircraft carrier when she bombed Hiroshima."

Anyone looking at Gale could tell he was incommunicado seeing the whole original landing, and take off in his mind. No one said the obvious: you're going to kill us and destroy this historic plane.

"Yeah, it mighta took off from one but it didn't land on no aircraft carrier afterwards," *said Casey.*

"Sorry Cap, but I believe it took off from an airfield, not a carrier. But anyway, in for a penny, in for a pound," *said Rocky.* "I'm with ya Cap." *And he started to hum The Battle Hymn of The Republic, right there in the skies over the rebel state of Virginia.*

• • •

I felt a little bad about the historic Enola Gay. Even if it survived the landing, no one would ever fly it out of there. I didn't think Arthur Godfrey, nice as he seemed, would want a National Icon and tons of tourists in his backyard.

"It's not worth it, guys," I yelled, too late to change their minds, "I have another way to be rescued. I'll go flyin' with the hawks." But then I remembered I wasn't on the airplane this time, in this story, and they couldn't hear me. At least I wasn't responsible for what they were about to do. The story was totally out of my hands now.

. . .

It was one of those Hollywood movie scenes with everyone humming along with Rock, as the plane skidding, skidding, skidding toward the drop-off, came to a precarious stop, teetering on the edge with the entire crew smushed up against the plexiglass nose shield peering into the abyss beyond.

"GET BACK! SHE'S GONNA' GO! GET TO THE TAIL!"

"What about you, Captain? By the way, great landing."

"Thank you," Rocky. *"I thought it was a fantastic landing too. Now I'm telling you, this old girl is going over the edge if you guys don't move it. I'll follow as soon as this damn seatbelt, correction, darn buckle opens. I've been meaning to get it fixed.*

Everyone made it out. And with a magnanimous gesture, to save an important American icon of salvation, the crew took time to pile enough rocks on the tail to stop the Enola from tipping over the edge, at least until the next big storm.

Arthur Godfrey wasn't around. Casey hot-wired the Piper Cub (he was from a certain ethnic neighborhood in Bayonne, New Jersey, and was experienced at such tasks). They filled up with fuel, and they took off back south, their goal: the meadow they saw near the top of First Cliffs.

. . .

As I walked through the trees toward the spot where I knew to start the climb, I finally cleared my mind of the Enola Gay. It was almost an impossibility, but it needed to be done. There was little danger in the climb itself. I was familiar with the rock face before me, but climbing is nothing that should be done while distracted. It was a huge reason why I liked to climb. You absolutely had to be in the moment. It was one of my passions. I had a collection of mountain climbing books, my two most precious: *East of Everest*, by Sir Edmund Hillary, and *The Ascent of Everest*, by John Hunt, where he lost his fingers to frostbite and never reached the summit of this: the most feared mountain in the world.

Both of these mountaineering feats occurred during my years in Virginia. And both books were among those ripped apart, destroyed, in the ransacking of my room that caused me to flee this institution that I knew deep down was soulless.

So, when I climbed, I climbed with that thrill and that respect, for that maddest of all human endeavors at my back, and the real distress I felt for the loss of those sacred texts, those recorded rites of passage for all of us that wish to understand.

When I climbed, I ceased being a boy. I became a human-animal facing a challenge to my very being. I climbed without any qualms or any aid from ropes, or pitons, or crampons, only wearing sneakers, climbing free-hand and with no one there to stop me, and no one there to help.

As I approached the cliff, the forest changed from deciduous trees to conifers, Eastern hemlock, which flourished in the shade cast by the cliffs and the moisture of the river. They stopped some fifteen feet from the wall where rocky breakdown from the cliff had accumulated. I never knew the actual height of the cliff, but more than a hundred feet is probable. I began to climb. Not difficult but challenging enough: a place that would be delighted to kill you if you were foolishly cavalier.

As I recall, the cliff ascended in a series of narrow step ledges with ten to twenty feet of vertical climbs between each. After an hour's climb, I was perhaps twenty feet from the top on a ten-inch ledge clinging to the wall, looking up to find the next handholds. Never good to hurry, I stopped for a few minutes and let my eyes drift upward to the view above, to rest them once more in the bluest sky before I continued. There in the sky above was a small airplane, circling lower and lower. A strange coincidence or a delusion. Either way, it was one I didn't need. I forced my mind to return its focus to the cliff.

· · ·

"I'm having second thoughts, guys."
"What do ya' mean, second thoughts, Gallin?"
"What will we do with him after we rescue him?"
"I don't know," said Rocky. "You're fucking Captain. You mean after four years—"
"Not quite," interrupted Casey.
"—after nearly four years of our lives doing this, you never gave that a thought? You're our Captain. We trust your judgment."
"Well, what can I say. Guilt is a powerful thing. It blanks out everything else. That's why people go to confession."
It's a little late for that, ain't it, Cap? Where did this guilt thing come from anyway?"
"Yes, it is too late. But that wouldn't work for me because I'm a God-fearin,' studying to become a minister by correspondence, Protestant. And I'm learnin' to love my guilt."
"But when did that happen?"
"All along. I've been listening to lessons on the radio on these here headphones."
"You don't want to save the twerp anymore?"
"Nope. It jus' came to me.... a kind of revelation. Being here was his God given destiny. At a certain point, everybody's got to learn to go along with the plan to get along. It just wouldn't be right for us to interfere with a Divine Plan."
"Oh shit. Well fuck me," said Rocky. " When were ya plannin' ta tell us about this?"

· · ·

Once more, fighting off the insistent nagging of my What-If story, my body, holding on for dear life eighty feet over the forest

I'm Not Here

floor, begged that I start to climb again. Another ten vertical feet brought me to a four-inch wide ledge. It was a particularly difficult section with meager handholds and almost nothing adequate for my feet. It was a relief when I was able to get my fingers over the edge of the next ledge and pull myself up. As my head cleared the lip of the ledge, I came face to face with a large timber rattler sunning himself. No more than ten inches away from my face, his empty black eyes were drilling through the back of my skull. Momentarily, we saw one another as two opponents sizing each other up before a fight. Then his tail rattle started. His head came up. His white mouth opened, four inches wide with two-inch fangs, tongue protruding, sensing the air, my air, and I watched him rear back and start forward to make the beginning strike in this contest I neither wanted nor was a fit match for.

How long does it take for your life to change irrevocably?

It doesn't matter; years or a second, irrevocable is just the same. I remember I thought about everything, truly everything, the absurdity of everything that brought me to this moment: from David's invitation to my earliest recollection sliding bare naked down a wooden telephone pole collapsed against my second-floor porch at the age of two.

I had a choice to make, get bitten and fall off the cliff or just fall off the cliff. So I let go. I wasn't afraid. There wasn't time. I slid back down the ten feet to that four-inch ledge below. I knew I was absolutely on my own. No one was going to come to my rescue. No amount of wishful thinking or even prayer would alter this reality. I lived more in that one second it took to make that decision and slide down those ten vertical feet than the accumulation of all my time at the academy one mile away or even my total time on earth. I was just another human-animal alive in the moment, trying to stay that way with not much to help me.

When my feet, really my toes, touched the ledge where I had looked up at the sky and the small airplane just moments ago,

I was moving too quickly to stop. I still was not afraid. In some way, it was just the next split-second thing in life that needed doing. What the outcome might be just didn't enter into it.

My toes, pointing down, compressed upon that ledge, and then the rest of my feet followed, and then my ankles, and then my calves and my knees, each in their turn catching up, compressing, then stopping while the rest of me, speeding by, instinctively pushed back against the ledge at that exact, correct moment and I found myself somersaulted, three hundred sixty degrees, head over heels, out into space away from the cliff's face as if I had practiced this trick to perfection many times and didn't need to give a second thought about its performance.

Was that really such a good thing? Now I was falling feet first with nothing to slow that fall. I glanced off the slippery edge of an Eastern hemlock tree, facing out away from its downward sloping branches. I struggled to grab hold over my head but couldn't until somehow, I got turned around. But now I was going far too fast, being abraded by the needles and the outer edges of the tarry branches, my eyes closed to protect them, my bare arms hoping for a chance embrace in this unrequited love need. But then I did get hold of a branch. Hugged it to me. Buried my face affectionately against its bristly surface. Still going too fast to stop, sliding-sliding-slipping-sliding toward the very end, then inexplicably, no longer falling,

I hung there, with my feet wildly searching the air for something solid, while gently bobbing up and down. How much farther did I need to fall to my death? I was too tired to hold on much longer. I opened my eyes and looked about for something helpful. There was the ground, two feet below. I let go, landed upright in a bed of accommodating soft hemlock needles, and stood where I landed for the longest time to see what possible condition I was in. My arms, hands, face, and bare legs were tattooed with minor cuts and scrapes. Tree pitch and needles covered all of me, in my hair and even inside my clothes.

Now what? How should I react? What was appropriate? I felt nothing specific at first. I hadn't screamed, not once. I was staring straight ahead. Then I smiled. As if bemused. I was!

I remember what I said then. I said, "Huh!" just once. That fall from the sky didn't feel like a rescue. It was a revelation. That's how it felt. I just didn't know what it revealed.

I found my way through the trees to the river, to where David and Charlie were still sitting, talking quietly. I stopped some ten feet away. Their backs were to me. They were not aware I was standing behind them. I watched them for some movement to see if I was really still alive or if they were real.

"You'll never guess what jus' happened to me." I blurted out.

"What?" one of them said impatiently, without looking around.

"I fell off the cliff. Almost from the top!"

"Yeah. Right," It must have been Charlie that spoke while still looking out at the river.

I walked over to where they were sitting. "Look at me," I said.

"Boy, you're a mess. What happened?" said Charlie.

"I jus' told you. I fell off the cliff. I came down through the trees."

"That isn't believable," said David. "You'd be dead if you fell from the top of the cliff. You'd be seriously injured. At least you would have some broken bones. Did you scream? We never heard anything. You would have screamed if you fell from the cliff. No, not from the cliff, maybe from a tree branch."

There was nothing more worth saying. I had grown used to my reality being denied by others. They got up, and we walked back to school.

Two weeks later, I graduated and didn't look back.

12

Westward-Ho!

Somehow, I managed to graduate from Shenandoah Valley Academy with the hope that that insanity was in the past. It was, and it wasn't. Turns out it was only the prep for the next even bigger event.

When my father came home with a new chrome and Formica kitchen set, I became quite confused. We lived in a thirty-five-foot Spartan house trailer, which had a built-in dining area. The set was tied onto the roof of our '49 four-door Dodge Sedan. It had been my grandparents car (my mother's parents). They had gotten a nine passenger 1952 Hudson limousine from the local funeral parlor in late '55. Obviously used too but in beautiful shape. And as my Grandfather John Whitehead, who never drove more than fifty miles in a week, explained, it was the car of his dreams. There were two fold-down seats, flower vials, and a roll-up privacy window between the front and rear seats. It was like an upside-down bathtub with narrow window slits and a hood that went on forever. Both Grandparents needed a large seat cushion and woodblocks added to the pedals in order to drive. Even then, my 4'10" Grandmother had to look through the steering wheel when she drove.

Since my return from boarding school, my primary task had been devoted to getting a driver's license. My father was teaching me.

"You're not concentrating." This comment overflowed with impatience.

I'm Not Here

I was.

"Don't you want to learn how to drive? You're seventeen. Every boy your age wants to learn."

Actually, I thought I was doing very well. We had only been at it for two weeks of hit and miss sessions, after work, when he wasn't too tired.

"I want you to get your license as soon as possible."

I said, "OK," but why? is what I was actually thinking.

I had just graduated from Shenandoah Valley Academy. If I wasn't giving my all to driver's ed, there might be a simple explanation: I felt disoriented. To my mind (and I had given this a lot of thought), I suspected that my being disoriented must be similar to what a convict felt when he found himself standing outside a prison for the first time in many years: I hated boarding school all the way to the bitter end. Now that I was out, I wanted some time to myself away from the overbearing four years of regimented living.

Well, it might be somewhat true from his viewpoint, that I was distracted or disoriented, but I wasn't quite standing around in a stupor, mouth hanging open disoriented, but learning to drive was not number one on my list for what to do after only being home for a few days. There was one occasion, though, when he asked, "Why are you standing there with your mouth hanging open, Jerry?"

And it was hanging open, but for an entirely different reason than being in a stupor. Call it serendipitous, but I was standing with my hands jammed into my back pockets watching him disembark from the Dodge when I asked, "Is that our kitchen set?" I nodded with my chin at the car. I though—*I hoped*—a reasonable explanation might be that he was helping someone in our church move: a charitable Christian act. Very communal. A "one for all, all for one" like Dumas' Musketeers and the nobility of purpose. Not, however, in character.

"Yes," was his response. "It's ours."

"Where's it go? I mean, there's no room inside the trailer."

"Let's go out for a driving lesson." He was a master at changing the subject. I recognized a teenager-ness in his switch-the-subject response.

"With that on the roof? Shouldn't we take it down?"

"No. It needs to stay there."

The table was tied on the roof upside down with four chairs stacked within the table legs. There was no roof rack, so the securing rope was wrapped through the rear windows then around, over and under everything making the whole chaotic mess look like a mangled centipede trapped in a demented spider web.

"No. I don't feel like it. Not tonight." Feigning fatigue, I started toward the trailer.

"Yes. Tonight. You're scheduled for your driver's test in two days. Give me a few minutes to get cleaned up, then we'll go out," he insisted.

"Bill. Jerry. Supper in fifteen minutes," my mother called.

I was saved. I went inside to sit down at the inadequate two-seater booth.

"Right after supper," he repeated as his back disappeared toward the rear of the trailer.

"What's right after supper, Jerry?" My mother looked over at me sitting in our lilliputian dining booth, and added, "Go wash up."

"My driving lesson... with that stuff on the roof."

"What stuff is that?"

"Outside on top of the car. A kitchen set. Why do we need a kitchen set anyway? Why won't he take it down?"

Being a teenager is never easy. Being a teenager in public with one's parent, mortifying. Being with one's parent when driving around with weird stuff on the car roof was even worse.

She opened the trailer door and looked out. "Oh yeah. I forgot."

"What?"

"Did you ask him?" She wanted to know?

"He wouldn't say. There's no room for it in here. He said it's ours, but where's it going?"

My mother smiled benignly and went back to humming over her steaming pots.

· · ·

Two days later, I failed my driver's test. The next appointment was in another three weeks. Several days later, without warning, we left on a long trip to see some friends of theirs in California. The kitchen set, I was finally told, would make it possible to stop along the road to eat without stopping in restaurants. This I learned on the first day, lying atop a pile of luggage so large it filled the rear of our car up to the rim of the front seats with the securing ropes still through the widows. And that is how I made the entire trip west. There was room for me to sit snugly between them on the bench seat up front, but I'd rather have been tied on the roof with the kitchen set than be in partial or even minimal physical contact with either of them. My father drove hunched over the wheel whistling tunelessly just under his breath while squinting at the road as if it was a vaporous illusion, while my mother hummed, almost audibly, fragments of songs back to back, while I checked out passengers in other vehicles to see if they saw me lying even with the back windows.

· · ·

Until the age of eleven, my mother and I had been best friends, my father a sporadic miasma of a presence. Then my father stopped drinking and got religion, and for the next two years, my mother became my ally in the struggle against my father's sudden intruding awareness that we existed. And then she capitulated and became a vapor while I went on without friend or ally in the struggle to be myself. For a while.

JERRY VIS

The first night out, we stopped in New Market, Virginia, the location of my years of incarceration at Shenandoah Valley Academy. The next night we made it to Alabama and the next to Texas. The weather was humid and hot, and our '49 Dodge had no air conditioning. It had been a strenuous push to reach Texas on the third day. Eastern Texas coming out of Louisiana was forested rolling hills, which soon gave way to flat open plains country. We were headed across the state at its widest, hottest, most arid point. At least, it looked like a desert to someone like me from the State of New Jersey. Why my father chose to take the southern route west in the summer was proving to be disastrous. It was because of the kitchen set on the roof of the car he told me: with the rope through the windows, they couldn't be closed all the way. So, going the southern route would be dryer, thus no chance of rain getting in the car. The moment we reached the plains, we ran into torrential rain. I and the luggage got soaked. The trip became a forced march to outrun the rain and the heat. My mother suggested we stop for the night. Maybe find an air-conditioned motel, dry out the luggage and get a bite to eat. We drove on.

Sometime around two in the morning, just west of Dallas, my father pulled over and said, "Jerry, you're driving."

I tried to remind him, "I've only got a learner's permit."

"And who's fault is that?"

At last, I understood his need for me to have a license. My mother didn't drive.

We were now in the middle of God's (abandoned) Country with endless barbed wire fencing, tumbleweed, and nary a person, town, diner, or motel in sight.

"Just for a couple of hours. Then I'll take over again."

It never occurred to me to tell him he was crazy, that I was scared. That this was going to be my first-time driving... It was nighttime... There were big trucks... And why didn't my mother say anything? Oh. She was asleep. Why not just pull over for a while?

I'm Not Here

"Just stay at the speed limit and look down to the right when headlights are coming toward you."

He moved over, and I slid in behind the wheel, sitting as far to the left as possible so I wouldn't come in contact with him.

Many, many hours and several stops for gas later, and aching from sitting semi-sideways so long, I passed through the Texas-New Mexico border outside El Paso with both parents still asleep. Running on fumes, I pulled into a café to get gas and something to eat. They both woke up and followed me single file into the café. No one said anything. We ate in a trance-like silence, got back in the car and drove off.

After finding out where we were (Santa Teresa, New Mexico), my mother put her foot down. By nature, my mother, a sweet-tempered woman of simple needs, asked little of life: creature comforts, good friends, and a happy home.

"I want to do something besides get to California. Isn't the Grand Canyon around here somewhere?"

"Yeah. In Arizona," I jumped in, "And the Petrified Forest too. Can we see both of them?" I asked.

My father, unwilling to relinquish any control, said, "You know I told Walter Hagar I'd be there in another two days."

That was of no interest to my mother. She let it be known that she intended to sleep in a bed that night, take a shower, eat in a restaurant and see some sites by getting out of the car. As for the kitchen set on top of the car, we only stopped once to take it down and use it. It took an hour to remove and replace.

He miraculously abandoned our path west and turned north. That night we slept in a motel just outside The Petrified National Forest.

"This is awful dry around here. It's desert. Where's this forest?" he asked.

This was more than I could ever have wanted. My father had no idea that the "forest" was a forest of huge fossilized trees. He was a believer in the Biblical six-day creation story, and while I was a baptized Christian, I could never get my brain around that explanation: too much of a stretch. I had the suspicion that science had chipped away at that answer to the unknown long ago.

The next day we were up at first light, ate a quick breakfast, again in a restaurant, and drove to the park.

We were the first to enter the park for the day. As there were no guided tours, we were given a park map to follow. A trail meandered off from the ranger's station into the desert with occasional signs along the way to explain what had taken place over tens of millions of eons of years to produce the incredibleness of what we were looking at: a forest that cast lots of light on the earth's past but no cooling shade for my father's beliefs.

After a few minutes, my father, protesting strongly, wanted to leave. He went on and on about the unpleasantness of the park, the growing heat of the day, anything but what was really bothering him: the classic confrontation of faith and science. After fifteen minutes, I walked off, leaving the two of them. The last words I heard were those of my mother, "I've done everything you wanted so far. Now it's my turn."

I retreated back to the park ranger building, not without a slight feeling of remorse for not telling them beforehand what this place was about.

The station stood near the head of an arroyo. Off about two hundred yards in the bottom of this arroyo was a herd of maybe thirty wild boar, scratching up a cloud of dust in an effort to find something edible. After half an hour I decided to sit down on the ground at the edge of the arroyo to watch them in comfort. They were my first glimpse, completely unexpected, of the live wild west, and I was fascinated by the frantic greedy effort they displayed in finding food and stealing it from each other. Not a very memorable experience, until a lone male boar spotted me and seemed to take great offence at my sitting down to watch him and his lady friends. He charged full speed along the bottom of the arroyo, then up the steep bank toward me. Higher and higher he climbed. I jumped to my feet, began backing away, and wondered if I would make it back to the safety of our car. He looked to be about two hundred snarling pounds with large tusks. He was a few feet from the top of the seventy-five-foot bank, looming as large as a Sherman tank, when he stumbled and rolled, tusk-end over tea kettle to the bottom of the bank, landing in a heap. I sat back down, thinking that would end it. But no. Up he jumped again and charged the bank until, nearly at the top—close enough to smell him—he lost his footing, and down he went once more, rolling end over end. Surely, he must be dead. He lay there motionless, legs in the air. But no, in one gigantic effort, he somersaulted to his feet and ran back to his harem. I thought, now that must certainly be the end, but no, again, and this time with the whole herd, he turned and attacked. Up the bank they all came within feet of the top, and down they all fell. This went on repeatedly for another thirty minutes, up and down, up and down as I sat there apprehensively amazed and amused at their pointless but determined effort.

Off in the distance, I heard my father calling to me. I ignored him for as long as I thought possible, then went to join them and asked, "How was it?"

"Amazing," said my mother. "Trees turned to stone. I never would have believed it if I hadn't seen it with my own eyes."

"How 'bout you, Dad?"

"Not very interesting, someone doesn't know their Bible... I mean, all those signs."

He looked truly distraught. "Why did you go off Jerry?"

I couldn't tell him. I knew how he would react, and I didn't want to hear it, and I also felt guilty because I had set him up. "It wasn't as interesting as I thought it would be," is what I said, which wasn't true. It would have taken me forever to unscramble my thoughts. There was something about the petrified trees and those maniacal boars that rubbed against each other, something to do with the nature of time and space. A feeling of being outside looking in on a magical mystery, but I couldn't get any farther with those thoughts. "I found some crazy animals that tried to kill me. Really weird. Wanna see 'em?"

They both stared at me as if I were speaking in a foreign language. I looked back and forth at their blankness and realized that we three were in different worlds.

"No. Not now. Let's get going," said my father in a trance state.

Not *NOW*? Maybe next week or month he'll look at them? What did that mean? I really didn't care. It was just another of those dismissive things that adults do to children. I was seventeen. I wanted to sarcastically suggest we all sprint back to the car to save time. Back in the car, I realized the whole morning was all about time: the trees, the boars, my father's rush to drive away.

Our next stop was the Grand Canyon, which sent my father into a rhapsody about the Great Biblical Flood. And by God, it is an overwhelming spectacle. I walked off to distance myself from his rhapsodic ruminations so I could try to comprehend the incomprehensible. Some people need an explanation for everything. I wasn't one of those. At least not yet. I preferred to feel a thing on my skin, be overwhelmed by it. Open myself to it. I didn't care about the reason for the Grand Canyon. I understood my father's necessity to know, to pin the world down. But somehow, he needed to know before he had even formed the question. But I also knew something. I resented him for that. I preferred a world of mystery, at least when I was around my father. I had an inkling that each new experience had to be accepted on its own terms. Not fit into a preconceived set of concepts but added to the pile of life to flavor everything the way seasoning does food.

I stopped along a low stonewall and placed my hands on either side of my face to screen out other people, the smooth sidewalks, and the stone wall itself, so I could feel as small and singular and vulnerable as I really was, to maybe—*maybe*—comprehend this place stretched out to the horizon before me. It felt as though there wasn't enough time in my entire life to become one with the view spread out before me. I got back in the car with that delicious incompleteness permanently a part of me.

. . .

We did the next five hundred miles without a stop and arrived in Thousand Oaks, California, fourteen hours later. Thousand Oaks, home of Jungleland, an early theme park where Tarzan and Robinhood movies were filmed in the forties and fifties. It was also home to the trailer park where we found the Hagars.

Walter Hagar, his wife, and their two kids lived in a boxy house trailer that was too small for their needs. We stayed with them for more than two months.

Walter was the son of the man that had converted my father to Adventism back in Paterson, New Jersey. We, or at least I, had never laid eyes on Walter or ever spoken to him. Didn't even know he existed. What we were doing there in this compact environment made little sense to me. Though I didn't devote much thought to understanding it. What was there to understand? This was a world of my parents' choosing. It seemed incomplete, as though I didn't have all the information. So, I approached it like I did most things, absorbing it through my skin, with imaginary hands to the sides of my face to screen out what seemed superfluous. It's why I can't remember Mrs. Hager's name or the two shadowy children. What I do remember are the endless, incredible clear blue warm mornings: walking outside, looking south down into the L.A. basin at that giant city sparkly white in the sun, then doing the same at dusk as the days' accumulated smog obscured the city, completely, then worked its way up the hill, to overtake the very ground I stood upon as it wrapped itself around the trailer in a poisonous evening embrace.

After my every morning perusal of the L.A. basin, I would climb into the '49 Dodge with my father to scour, L.A. for travel trailer dealerships. After the first few days, my mother declined the offer to join us, staying in the Hagar trailer with nothing to do and no way to leave it, which seemed preferable to her. Not so for me. Anything to fill the long day's hours. L.A. in the smog and summer heat was better than waiting for the hazy sun to set each night over the back edge of the trailer.

I asked fairly early on why he wanted to buy a trailer.

"Oh, I'm looking for a travel trailer, not a house trailer," he explained, although that wasn't an answer to the question I asked.

"So why are we lookin' at house trailers too then, Dad?"

"Just curious. Just interested to see how much they've changed in the last twenty years."

Our house trailer back home was made in the thirties.

Two months later, we were still going out every day to find the best possible buy. His reason for getting a travel trailer was to save money on the trip home since his wife refused to sleep in the car again or use the kitchen set, which was still tied to the roof of the car. There was nowhere else to keep it. I was still sleeping in the car every night.

"Anybody seen my keys?" Bill Vis, my father, always kept them in his pant's pocket, so those keys being missing could only mean one thing, someone had gone into his pants and taken them out.

"I have them," said my mother.

My father's days had become routine: up and out early with no time for frivolous conversation. The definition of which was anything other than trailer talk.

"You have them? Why do YOU have them?"

"Because we need to talk."

"What about?"

"We've been here two months, and the only thing we've done – you've done, is shop for a trailer. All I do every day is sit here and watch T.V. I could have stayed back east and done that there."

"I'm doin' it for us!"

"You're doin' it for yourself as far as I'm concerned. I need to get out of here. Do something else." It was a voice from my mother's past that I thought had been eternally extinguished.

Now that she brought it up, I had to agree. If I had to see one more trailer, I'd set myself on fire for entertainment.

"Today," she said.

"All right, all right. But not today. I'm real close on a deal, and I got to see this guy today. Tomorrow. We can do it then."

"Tomorrow. For real?"

"I promise," he said. "Where do you want to go?"

I jumped in, "Disneyland. Let's go there tomorrow. Okay, Mom?"

"That sounds good to me," she said and, with a touch of defiance, added, "Tomorrow. Definitely."

"Definitely," Bill Vis said directly into his wife's eyes.

The next day was Saturday. The day the Hagars and we went to church, being Adventists. I knew the moment my father made the promise to go to Disneyland, it was a problem. My poor mother, in the heat of the moment, forgot. And my father, in need of that same moment, was willing to promise anything just to get out the door. I was the only one that knew tomorrow would never happen, but I kept my mouth shut on the off chance it might come about. I secretly hoped and prayed God would side with me and give us all a day in Disneyland. We all needed the salvation that a day of diversion would bring.

It didn't happen. And then Sunday, Walter asked my father to take him somewhere, to help him, something about his car not working, needing a part to fix it. What could Bill say? What could his wife, Roselyn, say? That was Sunday.

Monday, my mother woke with a migraine. Terrible things that plagued her all her life. So, it wasn't until Tuesday that we actually left for Disneyland at sunup to beat the morning traffic and get the most out of the day by arriving when the park opened at eight.

L.A., with a population of just under two and a half million on the day of our excursion, was a sprawling tangle of mostly low rise buildings with too many cars rushing to get to work at a place where other cars had just left to get to work where the other bunch of cars had just left. Something along that line I speculated, for it took us many hours to drive the eighty miles south across the city to the empty parking lot at Disneyland by ten AM. The lot was empty because Disneyland was closed on Tuesdays.

My mother began to cry. My father, as compensation for his grievous effort, found another trailer sales place to stop at on the return trip north. We didn't arrive back in Thousand Oaks until mid-afternoon. We never made another attempt to visit Mickey Mouse and friends again.

The next day Bill Vis was up and out early on the trailer trail. My mother and I hung around the Hagar place, trying for invisibility. As everyone knows, house guests, like fish, begin to stink by the third day. We were now into the fifth week in that sardine can trailer.

Another week went by. My father was gone every day from seven in the morning until six at night. I spent most of the time alone walking up and down the road that led straight up out of the city within fifteen feet of the house trailer we were staying in. There was nowhere to go, so I took my time getting there.

One morning I noticed the kitchen set was missing from the roof of our car. As my father drove off, I asked my mother what had happened to it.

"It's across the street." She was pointing at an old, detached cabin-style motel."

"Why there?"

"We rented one of the little cabins. We thought it was about time for us to get out of the Hagar's way. They've been so nice. We thought we'd only be here for a couple of weeks."

"Why are you renting a cabin?"

"Oh. It's real cute. You'll have your own little room too."

"Why did you rent a cabin? Isn't it time to head back east?"

"We decided to stay a while longer. Your father has started to work in Mr. Hagar's shop."

"You said this was a vacation we were on. All we've done is look at trailers for over two months, and now we're movin' here? Is that the real reason Dad was lookin' for a trailer? House trailers, huh? Not a travel trailer, huh?"

"I guess."

"When did this happen? I bet before we even left on this trip. Was that the reason for the kitchen set?"

She gave a weak smile and a shrug of her shoulders.

"It was his idea, right? Like everything. His idea."

"Walter had a job waiting for your father in his shop. That's why he wanted to get out here fast."

I didn't want to hear any more about the reasons and the plans and the explanations. I sat down in the front end of the trailer and stared down the road toward L.A. My mother walked back to the kitchen area then back to where I was sitting. She stood there behind me for a bit, cleared her throat, then walked away. I watched the daily smog building in the city below begin to creep up the hill toward the trailer.

She was constantly clearing her throat, and since we got there, wheezing and gasping for breath. A lifelong sufferer of asthma, this place was making it worse.

It was late afternoon. We hadn't spoken since that morning. I was still sitting looking at the place where L.A. was earlier in the day.

My mother got the courage to speak to my back, "You all right, Jerry?"

I couldn't answer. And I couldn't turn around.

"Talk to me."

The smog, as usual, was now over the top of the hill and advancing on the trailer. I was too depressed and angry to talk. My eyes were starting to burn as they did every day at this time. I rubbed at them.

"Are you crying?"

"No. It's this smog again. Why would anyone want to live in this awful place? It's no good for your asthma. I'm goin' home."

"Jerry, we're moving here."

"I don't like it here. There's nothing to do."

"Give it time."

"I don't want to stay." It wasn't only the place I objected to, though there was little about it to like. It was my father. I didn't want to do one more thing he cooked up on the Q. T. with no other concern than what was in his head.

"Give it a few days. Why don't we go look at the cabin tonight? I think you'll like it."

"No."

"You're not being fair to your father. He's doing this for our good."

"When was he going to tell me? When we moved into the cabin? Was he going to kidnap me? No. He's already done that one."

"He'll be home from work soon. Will you think about it like I asked?"

What? Was I supposed to make up my mind before supper? Wouldn't want to inconvenience anyone.

We were now standing two feet apart when I repeated, "Mom... I wanna go home."

There was a long pause. "We sold the trailer back east. There's no place to go." She reached out to touch me, tears forming in her eyes.

I wanted her to touch me, that five-year-old me that still lurked inside, but I turned and left the trailer and walked away just as my father got out of his car and climbed the steps to the open door where my mother was standing.

I didn't speak that night, nor did I speak for the next three days. I had been thinking in circles: I didn't have any money, no job, no place to live back home. Maybe my Grandmother would take me in. Maybe I should shut up and stay. I couldn't stay.

I'm Not Here

Impossible to stay. California was a nice place to visit—*was it?*—but I wouldn't want to live there. I finally quipped to myself on the third afternoon. No. I was leaving even if I had to hitchhike. I knew how to do that, and I'd do it without money too.

"I spoke to your father last night. He wanted to know why you aren't talking."

I studied her face but didn't respond. Humph. He noticed something.

"No, he didn't. You clued him in."

She waited hopefully for me to ask the obvious. There was nothing more that I wanted to say.

She went on, "I told him you were unhappy."

I wanted to walk away, but I didn't have the energy. I wasn't unhappy. I was numb.

"I told him you did not want to stay. And I told him I didn't either. My asthma…"

I didn't respond. I had given her an out – her asthma. I really didn't care if they stayed or left. At that moment, I decided I was going.

"He said we could leave on Sunday."

He wanted to wait a few more days to finish out the week to get a full week's pay. Much of the money he got for the sale of the trailer was gone. I'd have to see about Sunday. I didn't trust him.

We did leave on Sunday. My parents said their farewells to the Hagars, and we headed south. My mother's desire to turn this trip into a vacation surfaced once more, and my father agreed to drive down to Mexico. The plan was to enter Mexico at Tijuana and drive across the top of the country and re-enter the States at Laredo, Texas. That would make the trip home really interesting, plus it would save a lot of money since it was Mexico. Fortunately, we no longer had the kitchen set on the car roof, so we didn't look like we were desperately poor immigrants fleeing the States.

We drove around Tijuana for an hour looking for an air-conditioned shopping center for my mother. If she was going to be a tourist in Mexico, she wanted to do it in comfort. But this was 1956 Mexico. We gave up for several reasons: for one thing, we couldn't speak Spanish. Anyone we encountered that spoke English wanted to take us to the very, very good store just outside of town to go shopping. We were naive but not that naive. The two individuals we met looked bad and smelled worse. We parked on the main street, which was lined with shoddy tourist shops, battered cars and donkey carts, and multiple street walkers, who tried to pull my father and me off the street into sleazy-looking rooming houses. My mother's comfort level breached, she suggested we find a place for a cup of coffee. I knew immediately what she had in mind. It was Popewynies Luncheonette down the street for our old house on North Main Street in Paterson, New Jersey. Oh well. After another pointless hour of searching for the nonexistent, we were back in the car heading east along the border with my mother once more in tears.

"Come on, Mom. Don't cry."

"I just wanted to go to a nice store. Get a nice cuppa cawfee."

"Mom, we're in Mexico. It's different here."

Her husband said impatiently, "This was your idea." He was only speaking to us in clipped sentences, and he was back to driving hunched over the steering wheel whistling under his breath. My mother had permanently traded in her humming for snuffling.

The only difference between the arid Mexican countryside and the arid Southwest border States was numerous wooden crosses every mile or so along this two-lane road.

"They must be some kind of highway marker," my father speculated. I've never seen anything like it back home.

"Why would they use crosses for highway markers," asked my mother.

"It is a Catholic country," I offered. "Did you notice the last one had flowers by it? Here comes another one. Let's stop, Dad."

The next cross had several bunches of fresh flowers around it. We still had no idea what the crosses were for when a beat-up truck stopped. A man got out and walked across the road toward us with more flowers. We moved out of his way. He looked at us strangely as he knelt, crossed himself, kissed the cross hanging from his neck, and placed the flowers on the ground next to the wooden marker.

Bill Vis, in a flash revelatory moment, said, "It's for an accident. Someone died here."

"Wow! All those crosses we passed are for dead people? This must be some bad road."

"I don't understand any of this," said Roselyn, "I want to go home, Bill. As fast as possible."

When we reached Mexicali, we crossed back into California and four days later parked the car in front of my Uncle Pete's house on Lafayette Street in Paterson. It was raining. It was the first rain I had seen since Texas, and it felt so good.

13

An Opposing Opined Opinion

Autumn, 1956

There is, of course, physical pain, and then there is mental anguish. It would have been better for all concerned if everyone had two broken legs

It wasn't in my father's nature to get a second opinion. Not because of overconfidence, but impulsiveness. Ran in the family. His brother Pete was the same. Even worse. And it was a realization I came to early on, by the age of eleven. Maybe if my father had told me what he wanted to do, move to California, given me enough lead time, I might have taken to the idea. Asking would have been even better. Though he never asked his wife anything. Why would he ask me? I imagine he just came home one day from work with the full-blown notion, "We're moving to California." I wondered, did he also instruct her not to tell me, or did she just know better, not because he'd physically threaten her, but because she knew it would have been not just useless but endlessly contentious. Changing his mind was pointless, like trying to turn a battleship around in a bathtub. But somehow, without fully understanding why I reacted as I did, I prevented the move to California. She had helped me by making it clear to him, somehow, that with or without his agreement, I was going back to New Jersey. And I was. Not that I had any more to return to than my parents did: no friends, no home. I hoped grandmother would help. I was (and I knew it at the time as clearly as I knew my name) sick of him, consciously, chronically sick of him and maybe even his church (my church too, officially joined through baptism in a moment of weakness, which I occasionally admitted to myself). And my mother... I wasn't sure anymore I had to get away even though I knew I was totally dependent upon him. California had been our unscheduled test of wills, and I had inadvertently won.

Now, what was I, or he or she to do? We were now back in Paterson, living in the unfinished attic of my Uncle Pete's house on Lafayette Street. The space consisted of a half-finished effort on Pete's part to make a rental apartment. There were two badly put together small rooms, one I used as a bedroom, with a door that almost closed and one window that looked out on the street. The other room was a windowless dining area with a card table and four unmatched chairs. There was also an unfinished kitchenette, a makeshift bathroom, and an open attic space where my parents slept. We had to make the best of it with scavenged furniture. We had nowhere else to go. The trailer at Lake Side was sold. My cousin Phyllis and her husband were in our old apartment on North Main Street filled with our old furniture, sold to them when my father bought the trailer.

Of his three brothers and one sister, Pete was the only one with any extra room or inclination, for filial reasons, to take us in. It wasn't a comfortable fit for my parents with Pete and Gert, his wife. My father and his brother were only a year apart: best childhood friends, fiercely competitive to the point of pettiness. They were barely on speaking terms when we returned because of an ongoing dispute over a 10" TV set that had belonged to their deceased father. Pete, arriving late to the reading of their father's will, missed his turn in the family pecking order to select an object from his father's possessions. My father took the set he suspected his brother wanted. That ruckus, begun several years ago, was still fresh in my Uncle Pete's mind.

Things didn't go well for us. How could they with no place of our own, no money, no jobs, no real sympathy from any quarter, only an unspoken gloating understanding on the part of Pete's family, of my father's situation? This I understood, not by any chance overheard remarks but by that prickly feeling on the skin and in the stomach whenever our two families came together. Initially, the prickliness brought me a perverse pleasure until one night, my mother woke me in a panic. Behind her, through the open doorway, I could hear my father screaming and moaning, thrashing about in their bed in the unfinished part of the attic.

It had been a terrible few weeks. My father not having found a job was morbid. My mother, with no money left to buy food, was distraught at the idea of asking for help. My father was after her to go to her mother for a loan, and when she finally agreed, he turned against her. He disliked his mother-in-law intensely. She then turned his bullying and phlegmatic badgering back against him. She started complaining and blaming and nagging every waking minute of every hour of every day and every night. I heard her through my bedroom door as I tried to go to sleep, always delivering the last word of the night.

Then came his middle of the night break down in that unheated attic twenty feet away. I had no idea what it was. It terrified me. My mother rushed to me for help, like a child. I was no more capable of helping her than she was her husband.

I screamed at her, "It's your fault. You're nagging him all the time. Driving him crazy. And me too."

She recoiled from me, the look on her face unforgettable as if she had just been savaged beyond repair. I was now terrified by what I said as well as for what was happening. It was the worst thing I could have done, and I knew it immediately. She ran from my room screaming. Why had I felt no compassion? I remember trying to believe – you're only seventeen, just a boy, you're not ready for this, you're not at fault, it's not your responsibility. And I knew it was despicable even as I said those impulsive heartless words to her. It was too late, the was damage done. The damage was done.

It's so easy to manage when life runs smoothly. Some pretend they know what they will do and how they will do it when things go wrong. Not one of us knew that night. I had no idea what was going to come out of my mouth even while I was saying it, nor did my mother in her misplaced plea for my help. Only my father's call for help was momentarily appropriate that night. But I wanted nothing to do with his or her needs any more than I wanted to sit between them on the front seat of the '49 Dodge on the California trip. Because in the overall scheme of things, I felt this was a dilemma of their own doing. What a lovely luxury for me to think I had no part in this. All of what we three did that night is what people usually do—muddle through, rationalize and hope that life will never get any worse.

My alcoholic father's solution to his muddled life had been to become an Adventist, to protect himself, from himself. A kind of insurance policy that he insisted my mother and I sign on to with him. That night, the policy failed as if it were a worn-out gossamer wrap. And I had that thought too. At that same time as all the others, in a kind of grand firework finale, that ended with this fizzling thought: why was I unable to leave my room, even my bed? I lay there staring through the dysfunctional door at the two of them: my dysfunctional father in their bed thrashing, screaming, my dysfunctional mother racing pointlessly around the bed yelling for help. Yet I did nothing, heard nothing. Absolutely not a sound. It mesmerized me. How could I see them there, twenty feet away, and not hear? Something, some large lump inside me, felt dead.

Eventually, my Uncle came running, then Janet and Raymond, my cousins, and then Aunt Gert.

"I called the doctor," she offered, breathless from the stairs. When the doctor arrived, he gave my father a sedative, and everyone went back to bed knowing that life wouldn't get any worse that night.

14

ADDICTED TO BAD BEHAVIOR

WINTER, 1957

I needed to bring the level of uncertainty down so I went to see my Uncle Phil. The visit became what I hoped for—a resurrection of any and all of our old political discussions. It was a moment of ironic recognition for me as I sat there finishing my cup of coffee.

My uncle, my first and only mentor in life, had no awareness of my dilemma, which was why I was sitting across for him that day. I thought seeing him would massage everything unpleasant away. So, I let him soothingly rave on about some injustice of capitalistic America being perpetrated upon the unwitting blue-collar American public.

Just a few days before, I had given coffee up as restitution for my insensitive horrific behavior toward my mother, the night my father had his nervous breakdown. In the midst of that trauma, she came to me for help. Instead of helping, I told her she was mostly the cause because of her constant complaining and nagging.

My mother, once my best friend, love of my life, and protector against my father, had ultimately chosen him and abandoned me from the moment she had acquiesced to shipping me off to school in rural Virginia.

Guilt is such a pervasive thing. Inescapable. And the nature of my own dilemma left me nowhere to turn except this escapist visit to my Uncle, or so I thought. I wasn't old enough or introspective enough to understand what had occurred. I just knew I was unable to go to my mother and say sorry. She didn't mention what occurred afterwards. Didn't confront me or treat me differently. Yet, our relationship had shifted. We now stood slightly apart from each other. What really occurred that night was the instantly felt realization and recognition that I was disappointed in her, although I could not verbalize it. More than disappointed, angry because she was a flawed, needy person, no longer my loving protector, and she needed to come to me for help. But I wasn't able to give it. That made me even angrier because of my own inability. I was still her child, but I didn't wish to make the switch, give her the help she was asking for. I wasn't ready to be an adult. I was more than willing to wallow around in my self-unawareness.

My uncle continued on without anything more than an occasional grunt of agreement from me. I drifted away from the thread of my visit. I recall staring into the dregs of my coffee. *I shouldn't be drinking coffee*, I realized. It was a part of a bargain with myself to atone for my behavior and, at the same time, be a better Adventist. A seemingly peculiar solution, more like a diversion, but as an Adventist, I was not supposed to drink coffee. Amongst other things. I didn't drink alcohol, didn't smoke, was a virgin. What was I to do to receive absolution from God – give up the only vice I had? Giving up coffee accomplished two things. It assuaged my guilt for my cruel behavior, though minimally, and it meant I was going to be a better Adventist, which, truth be known, was of no real concern for me.

Oh well, to hell with all that. I really liked coffee. And if I was willing to drink coffee at all, in spite of those self-imposed restrictions, including those imposed by the Adventist church, it should be the best damn cup of coffee on the planet. My cousin, Phillis, whose kitchen my uncle and I were sitting in, could not and did not ever make a decent cup of coffee: watery stuff you could see the cup bottom through. If I was going to be a disappointment to myself, it should be for the most black, thick liquid coffee that gave you vertigo just to smell it. My uncle poured himself a second cup and motioned with the pot toward me. Yes, I nodded. *Hell yes*, under my breath, though it was terrible coffee.

This room, the kitchen table, and the chair I sat upon were the same I'd used throughout my childhood. This was the house I grew up in. The place my parents gave over to my relatives, furniture and all, when my father bought the Spartan trailer.

The ivy-patterned wallpaper was the same that greeted me every morning for breakfast. Why had I needed to leave California so urgently? This return to my childhood world proved as poisonous to my well-being as the toxic air of Los Angeles. Most of my relatives were dead, estranged, or moved away. The children from my grade school years avoided me because I went to church on Saturday instead of Sunday. My old neighborhood was in decline, most of the shops vacant, houses no longer maintained, sidewalks no longer swept daily. Even this room and all the others adjoining it contained the furniture I'd grown up with. All had been sold to my cousin and her husband by my father, so he could buy a trailer. Only my communist Uncle Phil remained (the family pariah), a solitary relic from my childhood, and I loved him. But this visit hadn't worked the magic I hoped for. As I rose to leave, Uncle Phil finally asked about the trip.

"It was ridiculous," I responded. It was another of those things, like the harshness with my mother, that exploded from my mouth.

Phillis, in from the other room, buzzed the table with the coffee pot. I thought temperance might tone down my coffee guilt. "No more thanks."

"Your father's not well?" he asked, not waiting for an answer he already seemed to know. "What do you plan to do now?"

I didn't understand the question.

He added, "Now that you're back home?"

I'm Not Here

Four years before, my uncle had offered to pay for my college education after I graduated from high school if I would go to Russia to become an artist and work for the world revolution. All I needed to do was learn to speak Russian. He gave me the money to buy an album of recorded language lessons. He also tried to persuade my father, four years before, not to send me to a religious school, explaining that a good education taught a person how to think for themselves, not what to think. It took a while, but in time, I realized his belief in Russia was no different than my father's fundamentalist belief in the second coming of Jesus. They both thought they were exclusively right. It was crazy. They both possessed an insanity I couldn't, and in retrospect, rightly shouldn't have taken seriously. And yet, their insanity impacted me.

I took his twenty-dollar gift at the time and spent it on a fancy desk lamp because I couldn't stand the oppressive ceiling light in my dormitory room. He never followed up on his proposal.

"You don't like him, do you?"

This was the first time I had seen my uncle in three years. I was surprised that, out of the blue, he understood my internal turmoil.

"My father? No. I don't trust him. He only does what he wants. Never tells anyone, or asks anyone first, just turns everything upside down. He does what he wants. Always." I described the trip to California.

"Yes, I can see why you feel that way. Are you glad you came back?

I couldn't say.

"Or are you glad you left the West Coast?"

"Very glad," I said without hesitation.

"You did the same thing as your father."

"No! What do you mean? How?"

"You both were more concerned with getting away from something rather than going to something. That's never a good thing. Means you're looking in the wrong direction."

"My father was going to California, wasn't he?"

"He was, and he wasn't. And you were coming back to Paterson. How's that working out? I'd say not good since you're talking to me rather than your parents. Be better if you could talk to your father."

"I can't. I can't even stand to be near him."

"That sounds like something stronger than dislike, Jerry. What do you think the future holds?"

"I don't know. Go to college. But there's no money."

"That's an excellent idea. That's a possible plan with a future – it's looking in a positive direction. Now figure out how to make it happen."

"What?" I wondered if this was the same man that wanted me to go to college in Russia.

"If you want to really do something, you need to figure it out for yourself. Then there's nobody else to blame if it goes wrong."

"I can't do that. I'd need my parents to help me."

"That's partly true."

"How partly?"

"You'll need them to foot the bill. That's true. But where you go to school, what you want to become, that's your job. If you don't make it your job, you'll never be happy."

I sat down. "Is there any more coffee?"

He called to Phillis, "we'll take that coffee after all." In the same breath, he continued, "It means you have to be patient and work hard to make it happen. Remember, I offered to send you to school in Russia. I wasn't sure that day, but I thought you didn't want to do that. That's why I asked you to learn Russian so I could tell if you were interested. I gave you money so you would have no excuse for not doing it. What did you ever do with that money?"

It was a time for honesty. "I bought a study lamp for my desk at school. I'm sorry, Uncle Phil."

"I am too. I think Russia would have been a good thing, but only if you wanted it. How did you feel when you used the money in that way?

"I knew what I was doing, but I did it anyway. I didn't tell you because I didn't want to hurt your feelings."

"Really. That's what you thought – about my feelings? What do you think now?"

It was way, way too much for me. I shrugged.

"You made the right decision then. You knew you didn't want to go, you just didn't do it in the right way. Your father's an intelligent man. He's under a lot of stress. He's just confused right now. Remember, be patient, and focus on your plan. He'll come around."

Phyllis came over to the table, gave us new cups, and poured the coffee. I took a sip. We looked at each other. "I think I'd better go." I had an overpowering need to get away.

On the way home, I stopped on the North Straight Street Bridge and stared down into the Passaic River, and thought of all the hours I had spent down on the river's edge as a boy.

My uncle had made so much sense. His own life was one of chaos: divorced, one daughter somewhat estranged, constantly changing jobs and professions, always scrambling for money. Could I trust him? Was he right? If so, it would be the first time in my life that I had real, helpful insights. And from a "do what I say, not what I do" kind of person. I didn't think he was right about my father, though. He'd never come around. He was owned totally by his church. And for the first time, I realized my father's motivation to become religious was to escape his deadly alcoholic life. It worked for him. But what was my motivation? For anything?

15

HOPE SPRINGS A LEAK

FALL FALLOUT, 1956

The saving grace of one's lack of awareness is, you don't know how limited you are, which allows you to go through life thinking everyone else is the problem. Unless you get lucky and find out.

A few days after my father's catastrophic meltdown he walked back into his previous employer's office and asked for and got his old job back. In the same week, my mother started to waitress at The Copper Kettle, a sweet little sandwich shop on the south side of town just off Madison Avenue. The owners were nice, the tips generous. And at the same time, I got a job on an assembly line in an aluminum folding chair factory for a dollar five an hour.

I had planned to start college that fall. The California trip derailed that idea. Any money my parents said they had set aside for that purpose was used up on the trip. When we got back, we were all in an emotional meltdown with no money for basic living, let alone college. In the months preceding the trip, my father not only insisted I go to college, but he also insisted it be Washington Missionary College (now Columbia Union College), an Adventist school just north of D.C. in Tacoma Park, Maryland. Not my choice, but if I wanted to go elsewhere, I'd have to move out and do it on my own. That seemed an impossibility. I did want to go to college, but had no particular goal in mind

I'm Not Here

except to get away from a life with my father as soon as possible. My mother said as soon as they got back on their feet, she'd try to set aside money for school, but that I also had to help out. This was fine with me, anything to speed things up. So, I went to work in the hope that I could save money to start the next semester.

I found an ad in the help wanted section of the Paterson Morning Call, got on a bus that same morning to the edge of town, walked into the business office, and was hired. The factory was a grubby sweatshop though I didn't understand that at the time. I found it very grown up and exciting despite years of indoctrination by my communist uncle about the plight of the American factory worker.

I was placed on an assembly line, which consisted of a hundred-foot long table, three feet wide, with forty workers paired along each side of its length performing matching tasks to assemble cheap aluminum folding chairs. The business was in an old antiquated brick factory, unpainted, shabby, and tired looking. Bins of discarded aluminum chairs parts and rejects spilled from tallish metal garbage bins that lined the wall next to the entry. Hanging electrical wires and pipes, broken light fixtures, and cobwebs festooned the ceiling in an exhausted gray lace. A tall bank of windows along one wall, opaque with dirt, were the best reliable light source in this cavernous dimly lit space. The only accommodation available to the workers was a lunchroom of broken chairs and tables and filthy bathrooms, which completed my first foray into the mysterious, blue-collar world that was known to every father of every childhood friend I had but a fog of oblivion for me. My first day on the job should have clued me in, for every face of every worker had that same dead, glassy-eyed stare I had seen on the face of all the fathers of all my friends.

Instead, I took the job on its own terms, not making judgments or assumptions, just absorbing it, experiencing it in a strange attitude of romantic adventure leftover from my boyhood.

Jerry Vis

It was a typical eight-hour workday: it started at eight, with a fifteen-minute morning break and thirty minutes for lunch. The worker I was paired with was my age, a high school dropout, and a massive stutterer. He rarely uttered more than a few syllables at a time.

The demands on the line were minimal and mindless, so most workers spent the day in idle chatter, which, I suspect, slowed the line somewhat, causing errors while also keeping everyone on edge waiting for the wrath of God to descend upon them from the line foreman. One day, my partner disagreed strongly with adjacent workers and myself about our choice for the best Major League ball team, insisting through a mist of spittle, we must all be crazy.

Well, we weren't. We were all Dodger fans. A novelty for me since all my boyhood friends, at odds with my more Elysian tastes, were all to the man, Yankee fans, which required I keep my mouth shut. Caught on the horns of providence and with the support of my fellow linesmen, I leapt to the attack, intent upon releasing years of pent-up Dodger love. My work partner, incensed by our love fest that included denigrating remarks about Yankees, interrupted our outpouring, to our enormous surprise with, "I li... li... like the Yaa... Yaa... Yaa... Yaa..."

I matched his every stutter with, "...kee... kee... kee... kees..."

He was over the table, had me by the throat, and said perfectly, "Don't you ever make fuckin' fun of me."

He was much larger than I and could have pulverized me, but that was not the issue. I had it coming. I knew it, and I was mortified that I had been so impulsive and treated him so with such disdain. I felt exactly awful, the same as the night I said those thoughtless words to my mother.

"I'm so sorry," I said with everyone looking on. The whole line had stopped, and the line foreman came over to investigate.

Ronnie let go of me, climbed back over the table, and we went back to work. At lunchtime, every eye was watching us. I didn't wait for him to come after me. I went right up to him. He was ready for a fight.

"Ronnie. What I did was wrong."

"You're jus' afraid of me."

"Yes I am. You're much bigger than me. But I mean it. Please. I'm sorry. You were right. You have every right to come after me." There was a deadly silence around us and some snickering. I got out my lunch and said, "Let's go sit down together and talk." I didn't expect him to agree, but he did. By the end of our lunch break, we were okay with each other and ate lunch together from then on.

It felt good to make amends for that unkindness. I never told my mother I was sorry for my cruel words to her. I followed our family's traditional resolution to problems by letting them dwindle away into a dusty corner. "Less painful that way," was the unstated family code we lived by. Not really. Stored in the stomach, as time went by, was an accumulating knot of repressions. My mother was filled with them. My father, too proud, embarrassed, or fearful to work things out. So, people and things fell by the wayside: relatives, old friends, nursing wounds not admitted, till they became that knot in the stomach.

It was a time when communists and communism were center stage, reviled in our country. Yet, it was my chaotic commie uncle, eccentric to the bone, intelligent and at times profound, that told me, "Never hesitate. If it bothers, you deal with it. (He who hesitates is lost. I knew that.) But for once, he didn't understand my worry: "He who is lost, hesitates."

So, on my own, as an act of restitution, toward my mother and to make things right with Ronnie, I acted in a quite peculiar way. Besides publicly apologizing to Ronnie, which quickly defused that situation and won me a friend at work, I decided to privately extend my coffee abstention as a mental cat and nine tails for the cruelty to my mother. I should say, though, in the spirit of this writing, I never really did have a hard, firm coffee abstention. That abstention was a self-induced delusion. But I extended my abstention to going to the movies, reading fiction, eating meat, and doing Bible study lessons for Saturday church school each week. All firm requirements of the Adventist church. And in a euphoric moment of righteous generosity, I overextended myself by not skipping out on church services. This radical change in my behavior, I was sure, would be noticed by my mother and would therefore count as an apology.

If ever there was a goody-two-shoes in the making, I was it. My changed behavior bordered on dementia, an aberrant abstinence that got extended to include teenage norms as well: sex, cars, alcohol, smoking, Rock 'n' Roll and lying. Actually, there was no sex in my life because there was no opportunity, no cars because I couldn't afford one, no alcohol or smoking because they made me ill. One drink would put me draped over a toilet bowl all evening. I kept the two, which induced a modicum of guilt for lying and coffee, but then I figured I'd add them later when I got good at abstaining from the easy stuff. I got to the point where I took myself seriously and began to believe in my own gossamer wrapping of reform. Of course, there were fellows from church who were going to miss my companionship at the coffee shop on Sabbath mornings. It was a price (I hoped) I was willing to pay. All this left me with one nagging question: Why is what's evil effortlessly addictive and what's good such a pain in the... hard work?

. . .

Sometime in October, my mother found an apartment in North Haledon, and we were finally able to get out from under the scrutiny of Pete and Gert and my two cousins.

Now we only saw them at church, but with what felt like an increased level of disapproval due to the truncated time we spent together.

Our lives were now normal for people living on the edge: routinized and bare-boned.

I'm Not Here

One afternoon, the woman next to me in the assembly line went home sick. She was the third that day, and no backup person was left to take her place. The boss was frantic. He was considering closing down the whole operation for the rest of the day. Maybe even until those taken ill returned to work.

He was standing at the head of the line. No one had moved yet. I called out, "I can do it."

"Do both operations?"

"Yeah." I'm not sure what prompted that spontaneous reply, but I meant it and knew how I could make it work.

He wasn't so sure. If there were any problems with a chair, they usually threw it out. It was cheaper than fixing it, plus he didn't want to pay anyone if we didn't turn out the work fast enough. He'd be losing money on us. "Let me see."

He started up the line and stood next to me. I had no problem. All the operations were quite simple. The fact that I had to work faster made the time go by more quickly and was somewhat of an interesting challenge.

At the end of the day, the line foreman asked me to follow him to the office.

"I'm thinking of moving you to the prep area. Come in an hour earlier tomorrow. If this works out, I'll give you a raise. How old are you?"

I told him, "Seventeen."

The prep area took the aluminum tubing, cut it to length, bent it, and drilled the pieces for assembling. There was a person for each of these operations. I was put on the horizontal drilling machine. There wasn't much to it – place one end of a piece in the machine, step on a pedal to drill multiple holes, flip the piece over to the other end, do it again. There were four different setups required for the chair, plus I had to keep the drills oiled and sharp and not go too fast, or the holes for the bolts and rivets would be ragged.

Within a few minutes, I was pumping out finished pieces for the assembly line. By mid-afternoon, I caught up to the other two men cutting and bending tubing and was waiting for more pieces. The next day I was shown how to lay out and bend the stock. By mid-afternoon, I ran out of cut lengths to bend and drill. I liked this job, liked figuring out how to do it faster and better: liked racing against myself and the needs of the line. And of course, the boss loved it too but not enough. It was Friday. I picked up my pay. There was no raise. The boss motioned me into his office. "You're not doing bad so far, but I'd like to give it a little more time before I decide to keep you there."

Was he serious? I knew I was doing a better, faster job, and I knew he knew it too.

By mid-week, I was able to catch up to the person cutting up the stock by mid-afternoon. So, the foreman showed me how to do that job too. From then on, I did all the tubing prep for the assembly line.

That next payday the boss wanted to see me again. "OK, I going to keep you on in the prep department, and I'll give you that raise."

"How much," I asked.

"Five cents an hour. And don't ever tell anyone how old you are."

"Why is that?"

"You're supposed to be eighteen to run that equipment. You'd lose your job if the state inspector found out how old you are." And another thing he didn't tell me at the time, he'd get fined or even get shut down if the inspector found out my real age.

Not having the sense God gave to roadkill or a desperate need to support myself, I said, "I'm doin' three jobs. I thought I'd get more than a nickel raise."

"Well, those three men you replaced are still working here. I still need to pay them. There just isn't enough money for a bigger raise."

"Where they workin," I asked.

"In the new storm window department."

Without pause, I said, "I thought fifty cents more an hour would be about right."

"I can't do that. That's a thirty-three percent increase. You'd be getting the same amount as the line foreman. Maybe I can do ten cents. I'll let you know. And if you're still doing all right in six months, I'll give you another raise." Though he never specified what that amount would be. I thought, unrealistically, that I'd have enough saved in three months to start college. I wouldn't even be there.

In early October, the state inspector came to check up on work conditions. The line foreman ran over to me and told me not to talk to the inspector. "If he asks, lie about your age."

And he did. The inspector stood behind me for ten minutes, then tapped me on the shoulder and asked how old I was. The boss had just walked up to us. I looked at the two of them, a little too long, thought about my recent dedication to a better religious life, and lied. The inspector looked doubtful.

"I'm small for my age." I hoped he could see that I had to shave once in a while.

He squinted at the boss, then looked me in the eye and said, "Okay." I didn't think he believed me. The two men smiled and walked off together, back to the office.

Well, at least I'm still not drinking coffee... I thought. *...Yet.*

A month later, they switched me over to making aluminum storm doors where I had to use a large power cut-off saw, air-powered tools, huge pneumatic clamps, and a punch press. And then they shut the factory down just before Thanksgiving. The boss and his new partner told me they would be calling me back with a great new opportunity. I shouldn't look for another job. The week before they closed the factory, they told everyone they were changing the business and needed to shut down for a short while. They'd call everyone when they were ready to start up again. Just before Christmas, they called and asked me to come in for a talk. Said they were only going to make storm doors and windows in the future. They wanted me to be in charge of the door division with a few workers under me. I thought they were crazy. Even I understood that I was but a mere seventeen—and what that meant. Who would take orders from a kid who looked fourteen? But I thought I should see how much they would pay. The same salary as before was their offer.

"That sounds like a lot more work than I was doin' before? How about a dollar fifty an hour? That's only thirty cents more."

"No. Too much. You're just a kid. We can't do any more than another nickel an hour. We'll give you a good increase when the business gets going. You'll be up to one seventy-five in no time."

"No. I want a dollar fifty to start for all that work."

"We can't do it just now. Think about it. You'll be comin' in at the beginning of a real good thing. There's a big future here for you. Give it a week. We'll hold the job open till next Monday. That's a promise."

Monday. Only seven days away. College seemed like a distant fantasy. I'd saved very little. A dollar seventy-five sounded like a lot of money to me. At the rate things were going, it didn't look like I'd be going to college for a long time. My father had said that college was out for the time being. He needed time to recover financially, we needed to buy furniture and things for the apartment, and then we could begin to save money for me to start school.

I wasn't sure about the offer. It sounded like it would be a good job. I might be able to get a car of my own. A car would be nice. I needed to talk to someone. I thought of Uncle Phil. Communist Uncle Phil. He'd be the best person. He knew his way around jobs and businesses. He was still living in the second-floor apartment of our old house on North Main. I waited until Sunday and walked the six blocks to his house where again I found him downstairs at his daughter's, having coffee.

I explained the whole situation to him. He said nothing until I finished, then he asked me three questions: do they owe you any salary, did they change the company name, and why do you think they shut down the factory and let everybody go?

They did owe me my last week's pay.

"They said to stop back next Monday to get it."

"You're supposed to get paid Friday, right? Why do you think they made you wait? Did anyone else have to wait?" He took a long pause, sipped his coffee then continued, "You need to figure that out. Bosses always have a reason for doing what they do. Do you think they were out of money? Was it to make sure you'd come back so they could talk to you alone? Maybe they forgot, huh? What do you think? Now, what about the company name?"

I took a business card from my wallet that the boss had written their new phone number on in case I wanted to call during the week. My uncle called the number. "It's changed."

"What does that mean?"

"It means it's hard for anyone to come after them if they owe them money. It's like the old company died. It's hard to get money from a dead person or a dead company."

My response to the third question was, "They said they would hire everyone back."

"Do you believe them," my uncle wanted to know.

After a moment, I said, "No. I guess not. They're not making folding chairs anymore. So, then... they won't need so many people. And they got me to lie to the state inspector before, too."

"So, tell me, how does all of this make you feel? What was your gut reaction when they offered you that job?"

"Not very good. Kinda creepy. The boss looks creepy."

"I'd go with that," he said.

I clenched my teeth tight and squinted sideways down at the floor, and nodded slowly.

He paused, then asked, "What's going on with college?" He, as well as my father, had been prodding me in that direction. Other than my uncle on my mother's side sitting before me, I'd be the first one in my father's family to go to college.

I explained the money situation.

"Don't let that delay you," he said, "and don't buy a car. You'll wind up working for it. It will own you."

"But if I don't take that job, how will I save money?"

"You think that job or any job is the answer? You'll be a wage slave."

It didn't make sense to me. A wage slave? There wasn't any money. My grades were mediocre, so there was no chance of a scholarship. And if my parents were involved, I'd have to go to an Adventist school. Nothing worked, and nothing was making sense. I didn't even know what I wanted to become. Yet above anything else, I knew I wanted to go to college.

16

A Little Bird Told Me

NOVEMBER, 1958

Human mating rituals differ little from birds. This clever thought was crowding out a particularly tedious lecture on bird mating rituals in my Field Natural History class from which I had mentally departed in order to speculate on my own field natural behaviors, which were focused on one Betty Louise, who was for me a definite person of interest.

In general, the female bird feigns disinterest in a male bird's advances (Betty Lou did) while the male bird relentlessly puffs himself up, flashes his plumage, and does a dance to outdo the dances of other males to fend off their competition (I certainly did).

She was never available, would not accept a date. Plus, there were so many other males about, and I was late to the dance. I needed an approach that was likely to be distinctly different. I hit upon a cultural angle. I invited her to the Corcoran Gallery. That was my puffing up little dance, and I had a forbidden car, my plumage, that I was sure would put me securely in a class above any competition stuck on campus.

Plus, an added stratagem, I found out she worked in the library, so I applied for a job there, my scheme for out-dancing the competition. I might be able to catch her all alone in one of the study carousels or in the book stacks. This was not a carefully crafted strategy –more hormonal than thought out. To work in the library, you were required to take a course in Library

Science. My level of interest didn't actually rise above my interest in Betty Lou. A Dr. Weiss, the head librarian, taught the course. He looked and acted every bit the part of his plight in life. I fell asleep in the very first lecture and soon stopped attending his class. I didn't get the job at the library and so ended my end-run strategy for out-dancing the competition, for the moment.

I would love to boast how my outstanding intelligence and stellar grasp of reality led me to a menses moment of romantic achievement. Instead, I took a perceptive look at my prospects and carefully did nothing rational, which I now know, is a sign of a truly fervent mating ritual.

After Psychology class, on one gloriously warm sunny November day, I felt dispirited. My life seemed like an aspic salad: a variety of fruity bits suspended in a quivering lemon-colored Jello. I can't say that it resulted from that particular lecture that particular day or the unrelated flotsam and jetsam of events that described my dispirited life. It was more an osmosis of accumulated things. A subliminal clumping of random words and thought fragments during the only class I attended with some regularity that infused my aspic salad persona with a liquefying acid.

When I got to my room, I sat down on the edge of my bed and began uttering the word "dispirited" over and over in a singsong chant. It was a trick carried over from childhood. If I encountered something unpleasant, a reprimand or embarrassment, I would merely repeat the offending verbiage until it lost its meaning, turning it into a song: first high, then low, quavery, stretched out, until the moment and the word became devoid of comprehension. This time it wasn't working. In the midst of one of my vocal calisthenics regarding the word "dispirited," my roommate burst through the door and found me sitting on my bed, leaning back on my elbows, stark naked, head pointed at the ceiling lingering on the "R" sound with lips curled back to bare my teeth, growling like a dog. The momentum of his urgent entry carried him to a stop directly in front of me. He looked down at me.

I had been in the midst of changing into swimming trunks for a dip in the school pool when I lost my forward momentum and collapsed upon my bed.

"Rrrrrrrr 'm going for a swim, wanna come, Doug?" I added to the last growling sound.

Whatever urgent mission had propelled him into our room seemed immediately lost to history as he just as urgently backed out of the room. I listened through the unclosed door as his steps retreated down the hall, then returned to my therapeutic chanting still without success. I needed another word. Alternatives like dismal, retched, dysfunctional, lurking in the reptilian portion of my brain stem were just too harsh.

At that same time, I was reading the illicit novel *Great Expectations* and was swaddled in its thrall. So, although dispirited was a funny Victorian sort of word, I preferred it to clinically depressed. That was a most brutal term. Clinically depressed would have been more contemporaneous, but that term was too defining, even condemning, and indicated the need for years of therapy. In a dismissive act of avoidance, I was able to own up to my superficial shortcomings. I didn't fit the image of an over-sexed sports loving young American male, or, in the context of this bastion of aspiring academic saintliness, I wasn't a devout letter of the law Christian, more a wanna-be (but a sincere wanna-be) Christian, nor a dedicated student of obstetrics or some such obsessive goal with a secure financial future. Something I envied my roommate for. I was an English, or maybe History major. To admit I was depressed wasn't possible. In 1958 such things were unmentionable or unadmittable in or out of the world of the church.

In an allover general sense, the best I could do was acknowledge that I felt gloomy. But I didn't like that word any more than I liked clinically depressed. No. In all honesty, I disingenuously used "dispirited" to color over the big picture.

A piece of me, or more than a piece, it could have been multiple components of me, but not all of me, just enough that could no longer tell what bits worked and what didn't. Growing up seemed like no more than an accumulation of conflicting clumps of hormonal, cultural, familial demands, exaggerated and constricted by this campus utopia on the outskirts of D.C. And it was now my job to make sense of it? Put it together? Demonstrate competence? I didn't feel comfortable in my own skin. Where was I in all this? Where was I? Where was I? Where was I?

My presence, in, at, or during most school activities, was now declining rapidly. A situation I chose not to acknowledge. If only I had a comforting addiction: chain-smoking cigarettes, drinking beer by the case, gambling, whoring around, even praying a lot. Instead, I fell back on my recently acquired taste for art—implanted in me at the National Gallery that previous spring, which was the very first time I had ever visited an art museum. It proved to be a revelation.

Really! There's no accounting for escapist predilections under stress.

Maybe a career in art history would pull everything together, and I would forge ahead with purpose and focus. I could become a museum guard, which at the age of nineteen was a step forward over becoming a fireman at the age of five. I decided to take the one and only art class in the WMC curriculum. It met at night in the attic of the main classroom building. On the classroom wall hung a prominently displayed reproduction portrait of Jesus painted by Harry Anderson, an Adventist. It was a portrait of a dreamy-looking Scandinavian Christ with eyes upturned toward heaven. I had seen this painting many times before in various Adventist churches and always had the same instant perverse reaction: that of an alternative portrait of a short, swarthy, excessively hairy male, dressed in a ragged, dirty robe, weather-worn and haggard from living life on the run dodging Roman authorities, sleeping and living out of doors. A needed touch of reality, I thought, that left me feeling slightly uncomfortable. For I realized that in this picture by Mr. Anderson, man was not created in God's image as found in the book of Genesis, but God was created in man's image. I tried not to look at Harry Anderson's depiction. Repeatedly.

We students were given a box of watercolor paints, brushes, some 8 x 11 watercolor paper, and instructions to select a subject from the teacher's collection of landscape postcards to copy. The course consisted of less instruction than my seventh-grade art class in public school. That was it. I longed for a profound art learning experience. Instead, I got a teacher whose first duty was to ogle and flirt with the young women half his age, as Jesus, hanging on the wall behind him, diverted his eyes heavenward.

On some level, my education did prove to be minimally beneficial. It provided a kind of background noise of reverse stimulation. A decision to go to the Washington Cathedral oozed into my frontal lobe one day in the midst of a religion class lecture on the 2300 day prophecy of the Second Coming of Christ found in the book of Daniel as interpreted by the church. Which didn't happen, of course (the Second Coming, that is), leading to the overwhelmingly Great 1844 Disappointment. It seemed the Millerites as they were known then followed a Mr. Miller out onto a hilltop one night in upper New York State to partake of the Second Coming, which didn't happen. Seems Mr. Miller got the date wrong. Those that stuck by their guns in 1844 went on to form the Adventist Church, which, through the passage of time, came down to me at that school having my own fit of regret, or rather several of them, all of which I listed mentally as the religion class lecture wended its way: my dismal school work, my incompetence with the opposite sex, my phlegmatic religious dedication, a general lack of submission to something or other. My life was a hay pile of prickly loose ends. Each day was a mental befuddlement. I was also, in a conventional, cultural baseline sense, teenager-angry, terminally bored, and naive about the total absurdity that life could bestow on one. So, what better solution could there be than to go to the Washington Cathedral? *Really*, I asked myself. *Why not?* I answered.

Why not? It was a notion, no, a prescient impetus—a kind of knowing what was needed for my personal salvation. *Could I use that word, salvation, in such a self-serving context?* I could. And I would go to the Washington Cathedral because it was totally out of context because it was an adventure, a journey into another reality – I hoped. I had become an expert at escapist interludes. One day when I was twelve, I had ridden my bicycle from Paterson to the George Washington bridge, and on into New York City to be in control of my life. I had gone off climbing cliffs and exploring caves in Virginia at boarding school for the same reason –to be myself, find myself. Like looking in a mirror, an obverse reality, perhaps the real one. It made perfect sense, this notion or whatever it should prove to be, and at least, for now, it allowed me to miss the rest of that hermetic lecture on the origins of the Adventist church, which all of us in that classroom already knew.

17

It's a Lou-Lou

Winter, 1958

Here I was in a place I hated, a fish out of water, and the possible love of my life, Betty Lou, refused to accept a date with me. Ah... Tra La La...

"Have you ever been to the Corcoran Gallery Betty?"
"Betty Lou."
"What?"
"Betty Lou, not Betty. Betty's my mother's name. Actually, mine is Betty Louise. My family calls me Lou-Lou."
"Like Little Lou-Lou? The..." I said wrong-footedly with the other one in my mouth.
"... Cartoon character? Yes. Call me Betty Lou, okay?"
"Okay."
"And no, I've never been to the Corcoran."
"I was wondering if you're free Sunday afternoon. That maybe we could go there. Or to Great Falls Park."
"Okay. They both sound nice. But how'll we get there?"
"I've got a car." I realized my mistake. Could I trust her? I knew she wasn't flaky but was she a true blue church type – devoted to the rules?

She might ask, *How come you've got a car?*

"They're not allowed," she almost whispered, eyes wide and alert.

Feeling encouraged, "This place feels like a prison. We're right here in this D.C. suburb in this mess of dull houses and little stores. We may as well be in a desert or have a high wall around us."

"That really how you feel?" she looked concerned.

"Yeah. But all I want to do is get out into the country for a ride or go to a museum."

"Or a movie, or a bar?" she added.

She is suspicious, after all. "No. Is that what you think? I went to the Corcoran Gallery the other day," I said, dodging her question.

She relented, "All right. I'd love to get away from here. How 'bout this, if it rains, it's the Corcoran. If it's clear, Great Falls. Pick me up at the library at one. That's when I get off work there. Is that all right?"

"Great. Sunday at one?" I really wanted to go back to the Corcoran. I needed somebody else's take on what I sensed about the art, but, first things first. "We'll have to walk to the car. It's parked several blocks away from campus. Meeting at the library is perfect. That way, we can get away without being noticed."

She gave me a peculiar look, "Without being noticed?"

. . .

It was winter-warm and brilliantly clear, so we drove out to the countryside and hiked a short distance along the Potomac River to the falls—more like a gigantic rapid, but quite dramatic. I told Lou-Lou—still not able to get my head around an Italian girl with the name Betty Lou—about some of my more dramatic Virginia cave exploits along the Shenandoah River that flowed into this very same Potomac, which she seemed genuinely interested in. And how I fell off a hundred-foot cliff without getting hurt, and I thought as I said it, it must sound like bragging, but she seemed to believe me. And she spoke about her own hiking and camping out in wilderness areas, that she was a life-long Girl Scout, worked summers as a Scout leader back home, specializing in wilderness camping skills.

I, myself, a dropout from my Uncle Pete's Brownie Boy Scout troop after three weeks, was curious about this person's genuine admiration and affection for that world. There wasn't a single *esprit de corps* bone in my body, but I was savvy enough to keep my personal ineptitude to myself.

Otherwise, it was an innocent, sweet afternoon. We shared those simple direct things that people on a first date share with each other about family, likes, and dislikes. And though our details differed greatly, we seemed to share similar views on life in general. It was the first time I felt like I could be myself with a girl, just being uncomplicatedly myself. No pretenses. Well, almost none. Peculiar scouting issues aside, I made no feigned attempts at tailoring my comments and views. I wanted this time together to be honest, not as a conscious effort but unguarded. And she made that possible. We were both just nineteen and finding our individual ways forward, if not between ourselves, certainly in life.

I knew I wanted to spend more time with her.

Unlike myself, she was happy with her experience at school, studying to be a teacher. She, too, was a "lifer" as I thought of those born into Adventism but relaxed, not uptight and judgmental.

Hers was a split "lifer" family – mother Adventist, father not, but with no dissension between them. Except when it came to Mr. Hagar. Hagar, a self-appointed evangelical missionary, toured the countryside selling religious books, obsessively converting people (in my case, my father) and organizing new churches (in Betty Lou's case, her local church).

For some reason, creepy Hagar had decided to go to the church in Pearl River, NY, many miles from his own church in Paterson, NJ, and then managed to invite himself for dinner at the Pascale home every Saturday after church, where he'd only talk to Betty Lou's mother. Even asking her non-believer husband to leave the room so he and Mrs. Pascale could "discuss" church business behind a closed door. He was a syrupy obsessed fanatic that neither Lou nor I liked.

Remarkably, it was this same Hagar person that had sold the collected writings of prophetess Ellen G. White, as she is known within the Adventist Church to my parents, which resulted in the conversion of my father to said church and led to my agony at the Adventist high school. And now my internment at Washington Missionary College talking to, unbelievably, a person I was totally smitten with. None of this was believable. My God, but he, Hagar, as well as God, did work in mysterious ways.

Betty Lou went on to explain that her father, a very salt of the earth Calabrese Italian, didn't take kindly to this behavior and took it upon himself one fine Saturday afternoon to expel Hagar forcibly from his house. Forever. This left me with two strong awarenesses. First, not all "lifers" are cast from the same mold, and two: I hoped I would never have an issue with her father. Ever. And this is what transpired on our first date, which I received as a reviving breath of life in the lungs of my comatose life.

The winter day had turned damp and chilly, so we headed back to the campus. I felt whole and comfortable, not what guys, even evangelical Christian guys, are supposed to feel. Guys in their late teens are supposed to dream of nothing but getting into a girl's panties as soon as possible. It never occurred to me.

We hardly spoke on the ride back. It was the best day I'd spent with someone in years. It felt like a strap had been removed from around my chest. As we walked from the car to her dorm, she told me about the roommate she had last year, a girl from West Virginia, who revealed how fortunate she was not to have a smelly Italian for a roommate: this after I told her of some of my own experiences in boarding school, of being thought of as evil because I lived too close to New York City. Both of us laughed.

"Did you ever tell her you're Italian," I asked?

No. She liked the girl. Otherwise, she was fine.

"But your last name is so Italian, Lou-Lou."

"She'd never seen an Italian in her entire life. There aren't any where she's from in West Virginia," said Lou-Lou. "And don't call me Lou-Lou. It's Betty Lou."

I felt some of the reviving breath of life leave me for this social indiscretion. Just a smidge. But I had to do something to retrieve it.

When we reached the entrance to her dorm, she turned, smiled broadly, and thanked me for the pleasant afternoon.

I looked up at her, several steps above me, and without a moment of deliberation, said, "Will you marry me?"

I don't know. Maybe it was our relative heights. Being those few steps below put me at that traditional proposal height, kneeling before her. Had we both been on level ground, I'm sure it never would have happened, and right then I was wishing it hadn't. But then, deep, down, I really, really meant it.

She wrinkled up her face as if she had been overwhelmed by an unpleasant odor, looked me full in the eye, and said, "Are you crazy?" She then simply turned, climbed the rest of the steps to the dormitory porch and disappeared through the doorway without looking back.

. . .

"Did you take Betty Lou out this afternoon?" said Douglas, peculiarly interested in my sudden burgeoning love life.

I nodded.

"And?"

"We didn't get caught."

"What do you mean – 'didn't get caught?' Doing what?"

It was a slip of the tongue. I'd never revealed my car's existence to anyone, which left me with two possible answers to his escalating prurient interest. I opted for, "Never mind," then I turned away and for the first time that week, attempted to make my bed.

"That's not good enough. Tell me, or I'll get Nancy to find out what happened from Betty Lou." Nancy, Lou's good friend, was Douglas' girlfriend.

"Nothing happened, Doug. We went for a ride."

"Where – how – what happened? Did you get on base? First base at least?"

"No. We went to Great Falls, that's all. I borrowed a car from Pinky."

Pinky lived off-campus at home. His father had an auto salvage yard. Pinky was always showing up with different vehicles. It was a weak cover, I knew, but maybe he'd drop it.

"How'd it go?"

"Great. Really great. She's really nice. We went for a walk – talked a lot. I asked her to go steady."

"You're kidding? You know she's been going out with a lot of other guys. Murphy, for one. What did she say?"

"She said, I was crazy... Did you say Murphy? Who else?"

"Well, what did you expect? Of course, you're crazy. It was your first date. You screwed it up."

"Hey! What do you want? First, I'm useless because I didn't kiss her. Then I'm stupid for moving too fast."

"Yup. You got it."

"Maybe. I'll wait a couple days, and I'll go see her when she gets off work at the library. Please don't say anything to Nancy."

"I won't have to. She'll bring it up on 'er own. They're friends, ya' know?"

. . .

It never occurred to me to feel stupidly embarrassed. Never berated myself for asking her to marry me. My feeling was, *Okay, no big deal.* I'd just go on, patiently follow my intuition. If it was possible, it would work itself out in time. I knew I wasn't crazy. No doubt! No doubt there at all! It was just another of those moments in my life where I knew the outcome. And had every confidence that my proposal would work eventually, at its own pace. *No need to force her or scheme to change her mind.* I ruminated determinedly. *I'll just hang in there. I'll be cool. No pressure. Hold my cards closely. Keep my own counsel. Stay mum.*

. . .

"So, who else are you going out with," I asked her the very next time I saw her the very next day, in fact. "My roommate Doug told me you were dating Murph."

"Yes."

"Often?"

"Once... so far."

"Anyone else?"

"Look. We had a nice afternoon together. But in the last four months, I have had four proposals of marriage. Yours makes five. Is there something in the water? I'm not making it up. And I'm not bragging."

"I honestly don't think you are, and as far as water, I never touch the stuff." I forged ahead, "You free this Saturday?"

"I just started college. I need to get my degree. That's all I have the energy to do. It's all I want to do."

"We could go to the Corcoran."

18

Heart and Soul

I never got a handle on my love-hate relationship with the church during my stint at WMC. At the time, all the Do's and Don'ts became a blend of guilt and escapist wonder at the larger world, with a touch of young love slathered atop my twenty-some layer cake of confusion.

The moment I left the Cathedral I knew I would return. The immediate question: should I renew my invitation for Lou to come with me?

Dummy! If you have to ask yourself that question, you already know the answer.

In the meantime, I went to the bar with Connie. Connie and I had gone to the same high school and had sort of danced around the fact that we had both been attracted to each other back then. We had a couple of beers, talked about people we lost touch with since high school. She told me her brother had a change of heart about me. Things were becoming confusingly comfortable between us. I pretended they weren't.

"You promised to tell me about getting drunk when you were seven." She was pretending too. Or maybe she was going along?

"Aw. It's not much of a story."

"I don't care. I wanna hear it. Will you tell me?"

It seemed a safer subject than taking my chances on why her brother suddenly thought it was all right for me to be around his sister or where that might go otherwise. In the past, he had threatened me with severe bodily harm if I went anywhere near his sister.

But why the hell do you want to be safe? These words surged at me from the lusty end of my brain.

No, I've already got too, too, too many pieces from too many different puzzles banging around, came the prudent answer from, I'm not sure, someplace arthritic and reluctant that prudently went on... *You just need a timeout specifically on the Betty Lou, or even Connie, girlfriend issue.*

"Jerry. You there?"

"Ah, what? I mean yes. Yes."

"The story?"

. . .

I had every intention of getting back to the Cathedral before the Holiday break, but ennui ate holes in the days. Then it was time to go home. I made the trip in the old Green Slug, an affectionate moniker I had attached to my car, having to do with its inability to know where to take me whenever I needed to go for a solo ride. Ah yes. The green slug was a 1953 mint green, four-door Ford Sedan that would have been an embarrassment to me under normal late-teenage conditions. However, dormitory students were not permitted to have cars which gave me a certain status among those who knew I had one. I kept it hidden on local streets, off-campus, requiring I move it every day to a new location. This vehicle was my essential-mental-health-safety-relief-valve. I'd often take it out with no real destination in mind, letting the car have its way with me as if I were merely a passenger on a mystery tour.

But this time, I was fully in charge. I made the trip to my New Jersey home alone. I needed the privacy to put all things associated with school behind me. The act of driving would also delay or at least distract me from thinking about my arrival. As an obliquely humorous preparation for the trip, I looked up the definition of home. Of the many listed, the one I selected was "a place of origin of something". I particularly liked the "something."

The only memorable event to take place during that visit to my place of origin had to do with my Uncle Phil. After a large snowstorm, he couldn't find where he had parked his car. This was the second time this happened that I was aware of. The first time occurred when I was in third grade. That time, I found his Buick for him quite by accident while fleeing a situation I created in which both the fire department and the police were required. The car was buried under a semi-melted pile of snow with a handful of parking tickets on it.

This time he was on his own. I wouldn't have known this losing-of-the-car had occurred but for his one phone call. He needed a ride to the Adventist church! He was now in attendance... with his new Adventist girlfriend. My atheist, communist uncle was now going to the Adventist Church? The only advocate on my behalf against religious schooling was bought off with an Adventist girlfriend? I wondered briefly, how on earth that had come about? Then, I tossed the idea on the pile of unsorted puzzle pieces in my head.

• • •

And then I was back at school.

Lou was working the evening shift at the library, so I started showing up occasionally to walk her back to her dormitory at eight, three or four times a week. I was still fidgeting with the notion of asking her for another full-out real date. But not to the Cathedral. Affairs of the heart, I finally sorted out, should be kept separate from affairs of the soul. Half the trick to sorting out anything was to first identify the pieces. Those were two big ones. However, which puzzle they belonged in, separate ones or one big one would have to wait for a better day, or decade.

I'm Not Here

. . .

I went back to the Cathedral shortly after Christmas just to do a test run, to see if I would feel the same charge of energy. Since the last visit, I'd done some reading about the Cathedral's history. There were guided tours available, but I decided against that and went off to explore on my own.

In my readings, I learned that many of the European cathedrals were built on top of the sites of earlier churches: Gothic over Romanesque, and more interestingly, Romanesque over pagan sacred sites. My talent for perversity springing to the fore, I thought it seemed something like what dogs do to each other at fire hydrants.

The Washington Cathedral was built in that tradition of Gothic over Romanesque, and while I knew it wasn't so, I imagined an ancient sacred circle of stones beneath the Romanesque to duplicate the original designer's intent to replicate his European models of Christian over pagan. So, I was off to see what I missed before, the crypt chapels in the basement. Unlike the soaring, airy volumes of the main Cathedral, the Romanesque basement crypts, sheathed with glittering gold mosaics, were enclosed by low barrel-vaulted ceilings that made the space feel shielded from the outside world and solemnly ancient. Irresistibly beautiful. It should have, could have, been enough. But my instincts told me I'd come for something less tangible than history or irresistible beauty, though I'd no knowledge what that might be. I left for the day feeling what I hoped I would.

On the drive back, my mind, empty of any concerns, understood, that's why I went there: to be emptied!

. . .

It was another few weeks before I could make a return visit. Something else came up that threw me off stride.

The admission of one's personal inadequacies ranks right up there with cleaning cat puke from your bed pillow. Well, at least for me. Inadequacies, the few we admit to ourselves, consume a significant amount of personal mental energy on a daily / hourly basis to keep concealed from others. Teenagers, of which I was still marginally one, tend to devote volumes of energy to this task. My list, as I perceived it, was endless. I even created a mental file in descending order, of the many ways I did not conform to the Adventist or larger outside pagan world I found myself in. Most of this was typical teenage narcissism but, maybe most, were in response to the psycho-dramatic milieu of WMC.

My favorite inadequacy to keep concealed from my friends in and out of the church, was my waning interest in Rock 'n' Roll. I only listened to it in their presence to save face. And since rock was taboo at the school (no one was supposed to listen to it), it made my pretense easier to pull off. Except that the only value to come from this next event had nothing to do with inadequacies, but more usefully, the realization that life is a perpetual minefield of unintended consequences.

In 1952, I was as alive and conscious as any urban thirteen year old might be of the surrounding world when Rock n' Roll erupted upon the country. Forgive the profanity (in Adventist parlance), but "Judas Priest," I'd had enough of pop music drivel typified by "How much is that Doggy in the Window," "Shrimp boats is 'a comin'," or the likes of "The Chipmunk Song," by Alvin, Simon, and Theodore the three electronic chipmunks, in quivery high voices. The days of the classic American songbook, adult pop music that I grew up with, and loved, from the 40s and earlier, were over.

Initially, I was elated. *Wow! Fantastic!* is what I remember feeling when I heard Bill Haley and the Comets' recording of Rock Around the Clock, in the early days of Rock 'n' Roll, and then The Platters, and especially Fats Domino out of New Orleans. It's when the music descended into bubble gum rock, doo wop, and rockabilly a short time later that it lost me. That sort of music you could sing the instant you heard the first three notes as if you'd been swaddled in it since your infancy. Of course, it was about the beat, not the music, certainly not the lyrics either. I especially detested rockabilly, Elvis Presley, though I did purchase a pair of blue suede shoes with zippers. I thought they were really cool.

I know. I know. Bizarre, inconsistent behavior. Enough. I'm already in over my head. Stepped on the toes of too many folks' fond memories. Sorry but that fondness is just not mine. Except for Fats Domino.

It was Fats' vocals, with just enough syncopated laid back jazzy phrasing, that got my interest and led me on to Ray Charles and then The Hi-Lo's. That got me primed for Horace Silver, Dave Brubeck, Thelonious Monk, Peggy Lee with George Shearing, and then The Modern Jazz Quartet, which led me into classical music. I had had a short flirtation at the age of seven, lying on the floor of my great aunt's music room listening enthralled to "Bach's Concerto for violin in A minor," with my ear against the single large speaker on her floor model Victrola.

Which brings me to the time I was lying on my dorm room bed, hands tucked behind my head, staring up at the ceiling, when the Assistant Men's Dean for South Hall, Mr. Browne, burst through my door without knocking and skidded to a porcine stop somewhat winded—from running up the stairs—next to my bed, glaring down at me. It was the middle of the afternoon, and I was trying to overcome a mini-depression resulting from not sitting at my desk seven feet away, doing homework. And I was doing a gosh darn fine job of it too up until then.

Had I been from a Latin culture, this could have been me taking my siesta. No problem, then. But I wasn't, and it wasn't. Instead I was listening in rapt attention to the conductor Toscanini and the NBC Symphony Orchestra's recording of Beethoven's Ninth Symphony, the last movement, a work composed by Beethoven when he was completely deaf. Unbelievable. If there was ever a bit of anti-depression music, that was it, especially when played at full volume, which I was doing.

Classical music was a totally renewing experience for me, and I was thoroughly transported by the music to such an extent that the Assistant Dean's entry went mostly unnoticed. I mean, he was attempting to dislodge me from the choral performance of the Ode to Joy conclusion of the symphony!

In rapid fire, he said, "What are you doing, how come you're in bed in the middle of the afternoon, and why are you listening to that sort of music?"

In retrospect, my answers should have been getting mentally prepared to do my homework, taking a short siesta, and listening to this fantastic recording of the most revered classical work in the western world, the Ninth Symphony of Ludwig van Beethoven.

Instead, I said, "What?"

It could have been worse. I could have been playing Thelonious Monk or sultry Peggy Lee.

He yelled above the sound, "This noise is Satanic. Do you not understand that? No. I guess not." He walked to the record player on the desk and dragged the arm up off the record, scratching it.

I was now lying on my bed with my teeth bared in a-nails-across-the-blackboard grimace, and my eyes squinched up. I asked, sincerely amazed, "You don't like it?"

"You should be playing good Christian hymns. This noise is defiling the pristine Christian atmosphere of this dormitory."

I knew when any one of authority said the full word "dormitory" it was a really, really serious moment. Plus, I'd have bet my entire RCA record set of Beethoven's Nine Symphonies that he hadn't been at the performance of Britten's Ceremony of Carols, performed by the college's women's choir a scant few weeks ago. Not willingly, at least.

"I want you up and dressed in ten minutes and in my office with... with that... record. And why are you holding yourself in that peculiar way?"

I'm Not Here

Elbows in the air, hands clamped on either side of my head, teeth still bared, I responded, "Because you just ruined my record."

"Oh my," he said sarcastically, and as he turned to leave the room he repeated, "ten minutes."

When I entered the office, there were two men seated at Mr. Browne's desk, backlit by a low afternoon sun, which converted them into flattened black forms. I could tell from their voices that Dean Lowman from North Hall was to my right and Assistant Dean Browne on the left.

I looked around for a chair.

"Please step up to the front of the desk." The mechanical invitation came from the flat shape on my right.

"It's hard for me to see you."

Ignoring me, the flat shape said, "What's this I hear about your disruptive behavior?"

"I guess the music was too loud?" I said hopefully. "Is that what you mean?" I knew Mr. Browne had said "SORT of music," not "LOUD music."

"Where is the record you were asked to bring to the office?" said the silhouette to my left.

"Oh! Right here?" I brought it up from my side and showed it to them.

"May I see it?" asked Dean Lowman.

I extended it a few inches toward the two of them, not willing to let it leave my hands. "It's part of a set of Beethoven symphonies."

"You know, Mr. Vice, I have sensed a certain pulling away of late. I assume you know what I'm talking about?"

I shrugged slightly.

"I see. Do I need to explain that we are a close-knit Christian family here at WMC? Can I assume you understand that? It must be the major reason why you choose to place yourself in the embrace of this loving, supportive community?"

I shifted my weight from one foot to the next in such a way that I took a half step back from the desk.

"So, when things occur to disrupt that closeness, we become sincerely concerned. For everyone's sake." The Dean continued on in the same sugary tone. "This latest incident has made it necessary for us to talk to you, for your sake. It is not something we like to do or do lightly, but when someone's soul is at stake, and the quality of campus life disrupted by disharmonious behavior, we are compelled to act."

His arm emerged from his silhouette in an attempt to take the record.

I took another wobbly half-step back. "What? Do you mean, the music?" I was stalling.

"The record, Mr. Vice."

"Will I get it back?"

"It's not just the music," said the Assistant Dean. "You slink around like a ghost. I never see you. You've missed numerous prayer meetings, skipped classes, most notably religion class. What do you have to say?"

"I know. And it's been bothering me. It's something I've been praying about. I'm doing a little better getting to meetings."

"You mean you haven't missed any prayer meetings for the last few days? Not enough. Do you realize you owe over $100.00 in fines? And now there is this matter of the music." Now Dean Lowman had an impatient edge to his voice as well.

"That music is a total disruption... a distracting degradation of dormitory life. And it must stop," the Assistant Dean's silhouette cut in.

"You mean the Beethoven?" I was pretty sure that's what he meant, but I needed to know if he knew about the jazz I played. "I don't have to play it so loud."

"That's barely a sign of acknowledgment," said Dean Lowman.

"No. He shouldn't be listening to that kind of music at all. For everyone else's sake. It's a distraction. Mrs. White, our

I'M NOT HERE

Church founder, and prophetess, warned in her writings about such self-indulgent distractions. I think we need to confiscate those records." The silhouetted Assistant was now on his feet.

Meekly, I protested, "You can't do that."

"I believe I must. Do you agree, Dean Lowman?"

"You do what you see fit to restore a wholesome atmosphere in your dormitory, Mr. Browne."

"I just got that record for Christmas. It's part of a box set of all the symphonies." Overexcited, I shouted, "I'll STOP PLAYING IT. I'LL TAKE IT HOME NEXT TIME."

"Do you wish to be a part of our spiritual community here, Mr. Vice? That slippery attitude is exactly what has brought you to our attention."

"I can't give it to you. It will ruin the set. It was a Christmas present from my uncle."

There was a moment of silence then the Men's Dean responded. "For your own soul, you need to let go of such self-indulgent behavior. We want the whole set."

I let out a groan.

"This is not going in a good direction, Mr. Vice," (instead of Vis). "Do you plan to continue your education with us?"

"Yes," I said at a whisper.

The two men continued. Their words reached me as muffled sounds, for I had slipped back to the music room in my Great Aunt Tyne's house listening to Bach. I remembered the warmth of the snug, dark room that was off-limits to me at the age of seven. And how my aunt, discovering my illicit presence, didn't reprimand me but smiled and placed the recording of Bach's violin concerto on the record player and left me there alone to listen.

"This is for your own good," said the Assistant Dean.

The two dark flat shapes put their heads together, and then the Dean said, "We will not force you to surrender that recording though it would show your willingness to grow spiritually. It would be a truly convincing sign that you have taken our offer to help you to heart. Instead, here is what you are going to do. You will immediately bring your record player to this office. You will not miss any more Prayer Meetings. You will sign in and out anytime you leave the campus—you seem to disappear a lot. Plus, we will expect you to visit with Mr. Browne from time to time, whenever he determines a need, to let him know how you are progressing. If you agree to these requirements, this will not go any further. However, if you agree to relinquish those records at any time, we will welcome you back fully into our community. Do you agree?"

"What about my record player?"

"Oh, oh, oh... Do you agree, Mr. Vice?"

"I agree, Dean Lowman." Though I had no idea what "visits to show I was progressing" meant.

"Let me make this clearer for you. If you straighten up and make an effort to change, to fit in, you'll be able to finish your education here at WMC. Do you understand?"

"Yes," I said. And while my head understood, the rest of me wanted to know and literally asked, "Will I be able to get my record player back sometime?"

"*Mr. Vice...* your need for change has already begun."

19

Progress I Could Live With

I left the meeting with my damaged Beethoven record and returned without my record player. I then took the money I earned working at off-campus jobs (that had been intended to pay off my fines) and bought a new portable player. I hid it in the back of my closet. And whenever I left campus, I began signing out to places like the Jefferson and Lincoln memorials, the barber shop every week, the Smithsonian, the dry cleaners, Sligo Creek Park, a little too often for some places but just as I thought, no one ever said anything to me. And I felt angry, confused, and guilty in equally nullifying amounts.

"Where did you sign out for this time?" asked Connie. We were sitting in our favorite getaway bar in D.C. As good Adventists, we should not have been in a bar at all. But, for some time, we had departed from the straight and narrow, secretly of course, for our mutual mental health.

"A walk in Sligo Creek Park to complete a field report for my science class." I had just filled her in on my lost record player debacle.

"Aren't you afraid they'll catch on to you?"

"Yes and no... You ever hear of a Boilermaker?" I asked, ignoring her question.

"Yes and no. What's that mean? That's not an answer." She took one look at me and said, "All right. Next question. What's a Boilermaker?"

"It's a glass of beer with a shot glass of whiskey dropped into it. The whiskey stays in the glass until you reach the end of the beer. Wanna' try one?"

"It sounds like too much of a drink for me. Aren't you worried at all they'll catch you lying? Find out about your car? Or smell alcohol on you?"

"I'm gonna' try one," I said aloud to the ceiling. "And sure, I worry a little, but I check to see if anyone's following all the time. Besides, other than going to this bar, I don't do anything wrong. I work for your father, go for rides, I go to museums." It was starting to feel like an interrogation. "Anything else?"

"To start with, you're not supposed to have a car."

"There are buses. Mostly I sign out to places I can walk to."

"That's a lot of lies to remember. All right. Skip it. Tell me about that time when you were seven. When you got drunk?"

I was sorry I had ever mentioned it, but it was a better direction than the present conversation.

"My uncle and aunt were babysitting me one night. My Uncle was drinking Side Cars. That's a cocktail made with Brandy. He made one for me. Said it was time for me to learn how to drink like a grown up man. When my parents came to pick me up, I was drunk. So was my uncle, except I was sick and throwing up. My uncle told my parents he wanted them to clean up the mess and get me out of his house immediately. There was a big argument. My parents never saw them again."

"That's it?"

"Not quite. My father told my uncle that real grownups don't behave like that with children. That getting drunk gives kids the wrong idea about drinking."

"How you doin'?" She nodded at my empty glass.

"Fine. Think I'll have another Boiler Maker."

"That doesn't sound like you learned much that day."

"I was doing fine 'til you tricked me into coming to this place, Connie," I grinned. "I was a good Adventist, never had a drink."

"Is that all there is to that story?"

"You know, a real irony. There's more, but I never told anyone about it before. A little while later, my father came home so drunk one night, he almost died from alcohol poisoning. I sat up all night next to my bedroom door crying, scared to death, listening to my mother cry and scream too after the doctor left. She sat on the bed with him all night, waiting for him to die."

"Is that true? You can kill yourself like that by drinking too much in one night?"

"That's what the doctor told my mother. Said it was acute indigestion, and it was too late to do anything about it."

"So, what's the connection to your uncle?"

"A lesson. That my uncle was honest, and my father wasn't."

"That's a pretty weird thing to say. Your uncle did a terrible thing."

"But he didn't pretend to be something he wasn't."

Isn't that what you're doing when you sign out for Sligo Creek Park and then come here to this bar?"

"I guess I learned the wrong lesson."

"Is that what you really believe?"

"I don't know. All I know is that today, I needed to get away from school. That's all. And you? Does anyone in your family know you go drinking at a bar? Or are you lying too?"

"No. Not at all. I don't have to. Nobody's checking up on me like they are on you. They think I'm at school studying."

"Don't you think that's lying?"

She looked away and didn't say anything.

"Connie, you ever drink before we started coming here? The truth."

"Once. My father's not an Adventist."

"Only once? And…?"

"Next time."

"That's a deal. You know what I realized about my father and my uncle later on? They both were afraid."

"That's weird too. Both afraid? Do you mean of each other?"

"Just afraid in general. That's why they drank too much."

"That's too simple. Maybe they just like the way it feels."

"Well, maybe they drank too much so they wouldn't have to feel."

"About what?"

"I don't know. Grown up stuff. My uncle, as it turns out, was a crook. For real. And if you ever asked my father why he did that or if he was ever an alcoholic, he'll deny it. He's afraid to admit it. Why?"

"So, you're sayin' your uncle drank to forget he was a crook and your father drank because..."

"His life was going nowhere."

Skeptical for good reason, she asked, "You know that?"

"Take my word for it. I have good reason to say that. Drinking like that is like a kind of religion."

"What are you talking about? How is that like religion?"

"You know. Drinking makes you feel better, at least for a while. Only it doesn't last. Like church, you need to keep going back."

"You are really into a lot of strange stuff today, Jerry."

"Why do you drink, Connie? Does it make you feel better?"

"It's true. It does make me feel good for a while." She sounded puzzled rather than doubtful as if she had never thought about it before.

"But not Boiler Makers," I added. There was a pause as we looked at each other expectantly. I spoke first. "We can't do this anymore, shouldn't I mean."

"Why not. Don't you like this time together?"

"Very much. It's the best part of anything I'm doing... and then I feel guilty afterward." I didn't wait for her question. "I think I should be a good Christian and this—not you—but doing this is just what the church warns us about. Funny thing, a year of church doesn't add up to one afternoon sitting here with you having a beer." I was immediately sorry about what I said. Why I didn't want our relationship to evolve made no sense, but that was where I was. It was my spoiler talent for perversity or my own brand of fear.

She suddenly looked sad, but said nothing for a time, then added, "They're not the same thing: drinking and church. One is good, and one is bad. Right? You do know which is which?"

"I should take you home now. I can't miss any more prayer meetings."

The ride was silent until we were near her house.

"You all right, Connie?"

"Fine. I think I understand. About you, not what you think."

"I'm sorry, Connie. I just can't figure anything out. I need a break from looking over my shoulder. Maybe following the rules will help clear things up. You seem a lot more together than me. Do you mind if I ask, do you have any of these concerns?"

"No, I don't. Well, yes, but not as strong as you. There are things that don't make sense. You just have to let them be. Not worry them and yourself to death. Just move on. Things get sorted out in time, or they just fade away. There's always something new to take their place. That's what I think."

"I can see that, but it just isn't that way for me. For me, nothing goes away, it just gets added to the pile. I feel like I need a time out. Everything feels out of place. Let's not go to the bar anymore. Or at least for a while, okay? And thanks for listening to my muddled babbling."

I sat looking out through the windshield as she said goodbye and left the car. "I just had another weird idea, Connie." She bent down to peer through the open door. "Maybe people like Dean Lowman and Mr. Browne are scared too."

She shook her head, rolled her eyes, "You just can't stop, can you."

I grinned and said, "I'm on a roll."

"Yeah. Downhill."

"Thanks, Connie. I mean it."

20

THE NATURAL STATE OF BEING: COMPLETE RANDOMNESS?

WINTER, 1959

Is it the nature of nature to nourish, or is it the nature of nature to smirk behind a concealing hand?

Even though I bought a new record player, I rarely used it. I began attending religious services, stopped skipping classes, stopped using my car, stopped seeing Connie, kept mostly to myself, and slowly descended into a numbing state of disinterested gloominess relieved only by distracting obsessive thoughts, one of which was Betty Lou's name.

Using Lou's full name, Betty Louise, shortened by her family to Betty Lou, reminded me of someone I knew in high school that was from Dixie named Betty Lou. She pronounced that same name, BetaLeuw, with an upward inflection at the end. How could a girl from New York, 100% Italian to boot, be called Betty Lou? I was in love with Betty Lou. From the very first. It was quite literally an immediate recognition. My soulmate. And I, only nineteen years old, was certain. Oh, you hear about such things. They only happen in a story, or they're made up by gooey-eyed sentimentalists or stalkers. But it really was that way, though I wasn't sure it was the same for Lou. It didn't seem so. I'd just have to wait and see. But in the meantime, I was in a state of obsessive denial, trying to come to grips with the name. It was completely irrational. It was a bit like scratching an itchy healing wound, knowing you're doing yourself no good. It was, I rationalized, due in large measure to the fact that I had just spent several painful years in a rural southern high school as a misfit citified Yankee, and while I eventually adapted a veneer of southern mannerisms, I always felt that I was an itchy wound that wanted picking.

It was my problem, to be sure, her name and, at the time, my lack of southern comfort with it. But that name was disorienting and disconcerting. I preferred just plain Lou. Simply rolled off the tongue with ease and at the same time left your lips in a puckered state of kiss readiness. Whereas, saying Betty Lou required the use of so many mouth parts, no matter what emotion you began with, it became lost in the effort.

Murphy, who took her out a total of one time, came up with Belue, which I thought was really very clever and cute, but I refused to give my competitor the satisfaction of using it. It wouldn't have made any difference. Betty Lou insisted on Betty Lou, as was her right, and I never dared to cross that what-to-call-her bridge more than once if I wanted to be thought of as sane.

The bottom line to all this: I suspected she already thought I was insane.

...

All during the Washington Cathedral visits, the bar trips, and the Beethoven fiasco, I walked Lou back to her dorm from the library three to four times a week in the evening. I wasn't certain what my purpose was.

Perhaps on one level, it was the best I could hope for as a fall-back position after the insane proposal of marriage I'd made on our first date and her refusal to date ever again. A sort of keeping my toe in just in case she changed her mind about my sanity. There was a concert of Benjamin Britten music performed by the college women's choir, which she agreed to go to with me, but that turned out to be a one-off event. Maybe if I had followed up on my proposal to take her to the cathedral it would have worked out. But... I just didn't know why I didn't. Well, actually, yes, I did. Some nonsense I invented about the needed separation of love and soul. As if love and soul suffered from conflicting territorial imperatives.

It simply was Connie. Connie, Connie, Connie, Connie. I really liked Connie, and I knew she liked me, and Connie was willing, but we were not soulmates. This soulmate thing was really cluttering up the landscape. How many people on the plant had a soulmate? Judging from the couples I knew, none. Connie, Connie, Connie. I really liked her. So, what was the difference? After due consideration, which disrupted all of my numerous unoccupied moments, I realized Lou was a feeling in my head that filled up all the wrinkles in my brain while Connie was an intense visceral tingling in my body. So, what should I make of that?

As a bit of relief humor to smooth over my fledgling romantic forays, I formed a mental image of Connie and Lou as a Jules Feiffer, New Yorker cartoon balanced on a seesaw, feet suspended in the air, unable to tell which was going up and which down with the caption, It's not my turn. It most certainly must be yours? I don't want a turn, written in a balloon coming from both of their mouths. A kind of self-deprecating humor that gained significant relevance after my last bar date with Connie. I was sure I'd burned my bridges with her as well, that on top of being burned at-the-stake by the two deans, I was—not to be too overdrawn—feeling quite burnt out. Thus, walking Lou home, rather Betty Lou, on random evenings from her job was just enough intention on my part to give me an illusion of hope. Not so much about Betty Lou per se. But that there might come a time when the smoke would clear, and I would find a brave new way into a future that might include the opposite sex. This

I'M NOT HERE

was the kind of self-deluding thoughts that tiddlywinked into my reptilian brain as I continued my walk on autopilot back to my dorm each time.

After a week or so, the atmosphere of these evening walks began to change. How the walks began, I can't recall. She didn't ever object to my sitting on the bench outside the library waiting for her. And, of course, we began to talk. She'd sit down next to me, and we'd pick up on the last conversation. They couldn't last too long. Fifteen or twenty minutes at most, for she had to get back to her dorm before it was locked for the night. At first, we talked about gossipy things, but after a while, those items lost our interest. Instead, we gravitated to more substantive subjects: social issues, politics, history, and religion. I recall one conversation, which evolved into a significant religious concern. It began innocently with a question about what her father did for a living.

"He's an electrician. A member of the IBEW union. Does mostly commercial projects out of the local Rockland County Union Hall."

She described some of the jobs he did. One, in particular, was a pharmaceutical plant in Suffern, NY where he was the project manager for all the electrical work. The plant was very large and was being constructed to develop manufacturing processes for pharmaceutical pills. For years her father had been at odds with the union President over issues of how retirement funds for its members were being accounted for. As a result, though he was the most knowledgeable and skilled person in that local, he was never given jobs of higher-paying responsibility until the plant in Suffern. And only then was he selected by the local Union Hall because there was no one else available to meet the level of ability required by the company for that work. Most of the union workers sent by the hall to work under him were friends of the Union President. They did everything they could to sabotage the work, including leaving a large tool between two large live electrical panels in a special electrical closet. As job manager, it

207

became his responsibility to retrieve the tool. He had to squeeze between the unprotected panels, which could not be shut off, to remove the tool.

"All because he wouldn't go along with the Union Local's bookkeeping," she concluded.

"He sounds like a very remarkable person," I said. "A very honest, ethical person."

"Yes, he is. There were many nights when a large black limo would pull up outside the house with four men in it and just sit there for hours watching our house."

"What did he do?"

"He went out there one chilly night in a t-shirt and told them he didn't appreciate them threatening his family. I'm not sure what he told them, but they stopped showing up."

"Your father never joined the Adventist church, did he?"

"No. He never went to any church. As a boy, he went to the Catholic church off and on, but never as a grownup did he ever go to any church"

"Even though your mother was a devout Adventist? All her life? Even when they got married?"

"I know it seems strange."

"How did that work out?"

"He said if religion helped people, that's all that mattered. He often helped my mother with charitable activities in her church. Even did electrical work for the church. Never charged. Not once did he set foot in the church to attend a service. Never prayed, never said anything about the influence of his wife's beliefs on his children. Just said, like himself, when they can think for themselves, they will have to make their own choices. That's what he told all four of his children. Be your own person, think for yourself, and never let anyone tell you how to live your own life."

"This sounds like a morality story. I mean, I know it's true."

It was time for her to get back to her dorm, so we stopped there. Typically, I'd meet her after work at random evenings but the next night I was there, waiting for her.

"I couldn't get the story about your father out of my mind, Betty Lou."

"Really? He's just a father doing what needs to be done."

"I could tell from your description; you really love him and respect him. That makes him very special. I can't say the same for my father, but I don't want to get into that right now. But I'm curious."

"Why is that?"

"Religions all seem to declare that it is impossible to be a moral, ethical person without the strong presence of religion and a belief in God in your life. Yet, from what you said, your father was ethical and moral without either. Is that true, or did I not understand something? Tell me Lou, did your father ever say what his thoughts were about that?"

"Yes, he did. He felt that religions were exploitive and that if God didn't bother him, he would try not to be a bother to God."

"And you Betty Lou? What are your feelings? Do you agree with him? Wait. Before you answer that... what is he like?"

"He's gentle, firm, patient..."

"I'm sorry. I've no right to ask all this personal stuff."

"It's fine. Somehow our conversation just went there."

"I'm glad it did because this subject has been a great dilemma for me."

"What? How?"

"Do ethics and morality exist without God or religion? Do you think that is crazy?"

"The answer to your first question, 'do I agree with my father,' and the second about morality and ethics—I'm an Adventist."

And this became the pattern for our mini-evening conversations on any and all topics. No ruffled feelings, no taboos whether personal or philosophical, disagreements essential to the experience, and of course, absolutely no dating.

21

OH, DEAR, WHAT CAN THE MATTER BE?

The conflicting territorial issue between my soul and my heart continued though at that particular moment heart issues were definitely in the lead. That's when the Lowman / Browne dynamic duo reemerged in my life. I never saw it coming. I was sure I had made some progress in cleaning up my fitting-in-to-the college-community act and assumed my soul issues were just fine with the powers that be. But alas no. Again it was in the middle of the night. This time I didn't bother to dress. Instead I grabbed my roommate's bathrobe, my being unfit for public appearances and made it to Assistant Dean Browne's office where I was compelled to face those two men with gooseneck lamps blazing straight into my face. Within the first few minutes I realized my record player was no longer the issue. They had moved on to bigger and -no, just bigger things. I must concede here though that I had returned to my mental rehabilitation forays to museums and the Cathedral as often as reasonably possible.

What they wanted to know . . . That's not how they started. What they said was more declarative in nature- "We know you are smuggling in drugs and women of ill-repute for other college men."

"What?" That was my best and only response since their accusations left no room for debate. They wanted to know how I was procuring the above and where was I going when I disappeared all the time?

I'm Not Here

Well at this point I realize all you have, as the reader, is my word against theirs. And that's all I had as a defense. I realized we could have stayed there in that office for the rest of the night but I was tired and bored so what I said was "If you know I'm doing these things you must have someone following me when I disappear. You should get someone more competent to do that job then you won't need to stay up all hours of the night asking me to tell on myself. I asked to go.

In parting they assured me their concern was for my immortal soul. And oh yes, for the spiritual well-being of the larger college community as well.

• • •

It was impossible to sleep. My mind felt like a home for a stalled tornado. If I could have selected one emotion to experience it would have been the dreariness of another day of classes.

I had finally fallen asleep when Douglas began shaking me. "It's time for morning prayer." In a well-meaning good Samaritan effort he woke me of late, when he rose, knowing I'd procrastinate most of the morning away. Which was remarkable behavior considering how I often took out my frustrations on him. He was so decent and uncomplicated. We had become friends in a strange dancing-around-each-other's-differences kind of way.

"How come you've got my bathrobe on?"

"I'm sorry Doug. They got me up again last night. I couldn't find mine and Browne told me to get right down stairs.

I forgot I had it on when I laid back down on my bed."

"What did they want this time?"

"You'd never guess in a thousand years."

He had been on his way to the bathroom. Instead he sat down when he heard what I had to say. That day he too missed morning prayer.

Doug left for his first class at the last minute while I chose to spend the morning stranded in the darkened enclosure of my mind. It wasn't until early afternoon that I saw him again.

"Lou wants to see you Jerry. She's waiting at your usual bench out on the lawn."

"Did you say something to her about what happened?"

"Yes. She came up to me and asked where you were."

"Wish you hadn't."

"She asked if there was something wrong." "How'd she know that?"

"I don't know. You'd better hurry. She needs to get to work in the library soon."

It took another ten minutes for me to get out of Douglass's bathrobe and into my own clothes. I found Lou sitting on the bench reading.

Not wanting to dive right in to the topic of the moment I asked about the book.

"It's Thomas Hardy's Far from the Madding Crowd. Do you know him?"

Of course I didn't. "Where do you find these books you read. Is this one from back home too?. Mostly British novelists, right?"

Not fooled by my small talk ploy she said, "I know what they did to you."

Feeling reluctant I had been standing in front of her until then. She patted the bench for me to sit down.

"Douglass I suppose? What did he tell you?"

"That they called you a pimp. They said you're getting drugs for people here at school. What did you say to them."

"Enough to make it impossible to stay here I'm sure."

"Are you ready for that?"

"It's a mess. I'm a mess. It's too soon but I need to figure out what I should do. Maybe I should say I'm sorry. Start to go to meetings. It's too late to save some of my grades for transfer. That means I've wasted a good part of the last year, plus the money my parents spent. I should have dropped the classes I was failing so they wouldn't be on my transcript. Too late for that."

"If you went to meetings would. . . You'd need to believe. Could you believe?"

"That's a funny question. I suppose you mean could I be sincere? About what, my beliefs or them? I'm not sure what my beliefs are but I am sincere in my efforts to figure them out. As for them, do you mean I should try to look like I believe? Like them?"

"I don't think it's possible for you to do that. To look like you believe, not just believe?"

"I'd need to liquefy my brain either way. That's what I'm doing here any way. Isn't it?" Oh God I hoped she didn't think I included her in this.

"And you know you can't do it!"

"And now I know I can't do that!"

How had she gotten me to admit something so obvious for the first time? "But I need to try," I insisted.

"So if you could do it, go to meetings and start behaving in away that didn't draw attention, what then?"

"I know, I know. I'd still be very unhappy. But it goes way beyond this place. I don't know what I want to do whether I'm at this collage or another, become a historian or a carpenter, be an Adventist or a Hindu. I don't want to live at home any more. I'm sure Lowen is going to tell me to leave at any moment."

"I'm sorry. I can't talk any more. I've got to go to work. Please Jerry, let's talk more later. I get off work just before supper today. OK? Meet me at the library. Promise?"

I nodded agreement. "Thanks Lou. But it's not a good idea for you to be seen with me any more."

"Thanks yourself," she call out. "I'll see ya later. What are you going to do with the rest of the afternoon?"

"Go back to my room and think," I yelled to her.

Instead of going to my room I went to my car for some driving around therapy till dusk then headed back to my room.

Douglass found me lying in bed after supper and asked why I stood Betty Lou up.

"What gives you and everybody else the right to be in my business?"

"It wasn't me. She came looking for you. I promised I'd tell you. Seems like you've been mooning around her forever. Now that she wants to see you, you blow her off?"

"You know what she told me a while back? A guy named Bobby Stockstad, back home, asked her to marry him. He goes to Harvard or MIT. Some big school. He's going to be a nuclear scientist. I can't compete with that. Besides she just bein' real nice that's all."

"Why do you suppose she told you that?"

"That's what I wondered too."

"Did you ask her? How did that come up?"

"Are you kidding? Ask her? It just came up for no reason." I rolled over and faced the wall.

Other than an urgent need of the necessary room I didn't leave my bed for three days after that. Murphy came in to see why we weren't making our usual trips to the Hot Shoppe.

"Can't believe they did that."

"They did. I don't want to talk about it Murf. I need to figure out what the heck I'm doing. For that I need to be alone." I didn't say get the hell out and leave me alone but he got the gist and left. That was the end of day three. I hadn't eaten anything since the "nosey interview". I found it amusing to call it that. In some way it reminded me of an old lady back in the Paterson church. She had the ability to sniff out a person's inadequacies. She'd corner me between Sabbath school and the church service and ask questions about my Christian progress as if she had caught me fashioning a fine fabric into a poorly fitted suit of clothes. I wanted to tell her I have no talent for sewing. She was unrelenting.

By the fourth day I stopped showering or practicing hygene of any kind. I did finally take off the clothes I had put on the

I'm Not Here

last time I talked to Lou. Never bothered to get dressed other than underwear and just laid down on my bed. My roommate stopped talking to me because it was pointless. He stayed away as much as possible.

On the fifth day Hoyt, who would normally not have deigned to speak to me brought a tray of food into the room, set it down on the desk and left without a word.

Ironically escapist sleep eluded me. For days I slept in starts and fits, the worst times being the dark of night when sleep refused my every effort. No one came near me. Food kept arriving, most of the time without my notice. Neither Browne nor Lowen showed their faces. I sneeringly assumed they had no intention of taking up my offer for twenty-four hour surveillance. What I was left with, that circled round me like a starving wolf, were those thoughts I wished, with all my heart, would disappear.

The irrelevance of time became a permanent torment. I floated in a grey world that reminded me of the first memorable dream I had when I was a toddler. It began with me wandering alone on a featureless grey landscape under a lowering grey sky. There was nothing memorable other than a feeling of desperate loneliness as I walked without purpose until I came upon a young golden haired women dressed in a flowing gossamer gown leading a line of older children that I tried to join as they moved toward a trickle of light edging the horizon. Then all vanished but the oppressive greyness with me walking aimlessly once more and then the dream sequence began again.

This time the dream from so very long ago seemed prophetic. Why else should it emerge from that deep dark slot in my memory? At least it was a distraction. Was Lou the golden haired maiden, the trailing line of children my competing suitors, and I the last to arrive, unable to keep up, measure up? Certainly the timeless grey landscape was my present world.

So what! What good was any of this. Did I care what it meant? Did it mean anything was going to change?

Maybe there was another interpretation. The golden haired women was the church founder, Ellen G. White, the obedient following line of children, everyone here at the college, the trickle of light the promise of heaven, and me struggling, and then failing to join the line, my present dilemma that kept repeating to no good effect.

Well that's what occurred in my addled mind in my grim room after a week of solitary self-confinement.

And then, in one instant I came to an ironic conclusion about prophetic messages: they're what ever you think they are. Why not this one: the Adventist came into being, by believing that the prophesies for Jesus second coming pinpointed the exact year of 1844. When that didn't happen they choose to rework their calculations rather than re-think the basic premise. Simply put their view of reality was going to remain their view of reality.

Now I had a reason for being in that room and what ever it took I wasn't going to leave until I had a better understanding of my enervating apostasy. Was it of the devil? Or were Browne and Lowen for all their self-righteous pretensions the henchmen of Satan. Was this a new found freedom or a better trap? If freedom was the benefit of my new awareness, and I was certain it was, then giving them or any of this mini-world any importance by distaining it would sink me to the same level of self righteousness. This wasn't so much a concrete thought as a glancing insight that didn't welcome close scrutiny. I was about to see how my new awareness played out and soon.

Nothing changed. I stayed trapped in my room, refused to take care of my self, still ate only if someone brought food to me, talked to no one. People came and went at times. I never looked at them. So much for revelations. I sank back into my pit of despair as quickly as I had emerged. What ever had flashed through my presumptuous soul sank into that pit with me where I now felt the overwhelming need to get even. Inflict pain.

My guess from my bed lying on my back was that a bit more than a week had gone by. My mind was fried. My body ached from non-movement. But getting myself upright seemed insurmountable.

I was imagining getting one leg over the side of my bed when the door opened abruptly. Three guys and Douglass came into the room with card board boxes, gathered up all his belongings in one ten minute burst of efficiency and left without a word leaving me completely and utterly alone.

I guess he just moved out, I speculated dumbly. Was that good? Yes, I said to myself. Really good. Did I feel guilty? Of driving Douglass crazy! No . Maybe yes in a second hand sense, as if his moving out was a well-crafted script and I felt the painful guilt intended till the curtain came down and the door closed behind him. But in a guilt ridden sense? No.

Yes, yes, alone at last. Maybe now I could get out of bed with fewer reminders of where I was. Time to leave my toxic chrysalis stage, sprinkled into my thoughts. For in a miniscule sense I felt optimistic enough to rearrange the furniture in my room. But to what purpose, one half of my mind asked the other half. Wait and see. Just wait and see.

. . .

I pushed Doug's bed to the other end of the room in front of the closet door. Since I'd no plan to get dressed in the immediate future this seemed the best way to open up the space in my room. MY ROOM. That sounded marvelous. Next I moved the desk away from the grimy window into the freed corner, got out the unused paints from my paint-by-number sets and began to draw and paint on canvass board that I had purchased several weeks ago on a whim. The desk served as my pallet and the room's corner my easel where I leaned the canvass board against the vee of the two walls. For subject matter I used images from Doug's forgotten National Geographic Magazines. Though he did come back for them. I told him he could have them once I'd finished with them. He looked at me for a protracted moment then turned and left without a word.

The only thing I cared about for the next week was painting, any hour of the day or night. I slept in fits and starts, often rising from a catnap with a solution for a mix of paints or how to change a value to create a cast shadow. It was thrilling. Not so much the finished product but the process. Smugly I thought, a mere few months before I had failed the art course at the school.

The destructive tornado that had taken up residence in my brain a short time ago was now the driving creative force for every second I was awake. I hardly paused between paintings. Hoyt came, Murphy came, bringing me food. They voluntarily were keeping me alive. I must have seemed ungrateful, certainly demented, but the effort required to stop for appearances sake would have been far too costly. I never spoke. I barely ate. And unbelievably, they never stopped.

I managed to complete four paintings, nine inches by twelve, in a little over one week. Were they any good? I certainly thought so. But I wasn't sure if their looming significance was due to their excellence or a needed dramatic distraction. I wanted some one else's opinion. Lou had sent word via Murphy that she wanted to see me.

I pulled the bed away from the closet, found some clothes to wear, grabbed the driest canvass and left for the library. It was nearly nine o-clock in the evening. The library would just be closing.

A few brief minutes after settling down on a bench across from the library steps I heard, "Jerry! You've left your room!"

"I thought if you didn't mind I'd like to walk you back to your dorm, Lou."

Why I couldn't say Lou you are the only person on this planet I longed to see, but then, realistically why would she want to see me? But when she said," Jerry! You've left your room," it added to my new found feelings of hopefulness. It wasn't the words but that indefinable inflection in her voice, the arms that spontaneously reached upward in an embrace of the sky as she came down the steps toward me. Could that mean she was absolutely mine? A full-body-contact-hug would have been more conclusive but I was in no position to quibble.

"OK. But first tell me is that blue paint on your face?"

"Oh. I don't know. It could be."

"Have you taken up wearing eye shadow?"

"Not a chance. I am technically an Adventist don't forget."

"Well it is only over one eye. What is it doing there?"

"I've been painting."

"Your room?"

"No."

"It hard to believe you didn't leave your room for more than two weeks. Douglas said you had gone crazy. You wouldn't get out of bed. Wouldn't eat or get dressed. Wouldn't talk. He said he couldn't take it any more so he moved out. It must be true. Is it? And now you show up with blue paint on your face."

"I'm thinking of becoming a Druid."

"A tentative one, huh?"

"One eye at a time. It's a trial period. If I do well I'll give up being an Adventist."

I reached down to the side of the bench and brought up the painting I'd leaned there. ". . . been making paintings. I brought this one to show you."

She look directed at me and asked. "Are you all right?"

I ignored her question and said, "I hope you don't mind. I want you to tell me if it's any good. I thought of you because you know so much about art and I knew you'd be honest."

I meant what I had said. She would be honest. No one else in my life was. Not my parents, not this school, not the Adventists. All pretending that what they believed was all there could be. Not Douglass, not my grandparents that made me swear on the Bible, nor Connie that wanted something physical because she thought that would win me over. It almost did. Every body wanted what was good for them. I needed someone so very honest they would look beyond the painting to see the me that longed for a reality that included the Ceremony of Carols, and The Washington Cathedral and making art, making art! And Dave Brubeck and Beethoven and the Magic Mountain. And I knew it was too much to expect of her or any one. And I didn't care. Because it was what I desperately needed.

"Before I really look at the painting I'd like to talk first."

I hadn't considered that possibility. "I guess so. Is it because I never showed up?"

"Some what but also you seem changed."

"Changed?"

"As if nothing happened. What's going on? You disappeared . . . never said a word to anyone according to

Douglass. You really spooked him."

"I didn't know what I was doing. Not in a normal everyday sense. With my life. I just couldn't leave my room that's all. It wasn't like the last time. I chose to stay in my room in the afternoons. So I'd not be tempted. To find a way to be a true Adventist."

"Tempted by what? That was also strange. Were you trying to turn your self into a part time monk?. What did you think you were avoiding?" Now you've done it again.

"I'd rather not say."

"Is that because what Loweman and Browne accused you of is true? I don't think it is, but I want to find out what you were trying to avoid. And now, what ever it was that kept you in your room this time. You say it's different this time and I can imagine how it might be. But I want to hear your explanation. Something must have happened to explain the way you're acting now."

"Why do you want to know? What can you learn from a mixed up person like me?" I was really looking to see what her motivation was.

"Not learn. Understand."

" Learn, understand. It's still mixed up because there's what I did, then there's why I did it, and then there's, I don't know."

"I want to understand because you're trying to figure it out. You think about things that everybody else excepts without question. You like things that most of the people around here consider strange at best. Douglass said he doesn't understand half the things you do or talk about. Nor does

Loweman, so he imagines what they are. Do you agree?"

"Yes and no. He's partly right but he let's his imagination go too far in a narrow slotted kind of way, which is the exact width of his world. Lou, sorry but we don't have the time for this now, and I really want you to look at the painting." It was a conscious dodge to stop her questioning. I needed time to clear my conflicted thoughts before I could go farther.

"You're right. Tomorrow? After lunch OK? . . . at Halcion, in the dating room."

"Alright. What about the painting?"

" Since we're out of time and the light's not good here, bring it tomorrow. By the way there's no blue in this painting." "Twelve thirty tomorrow?"

"Fine. If you don't show up, I'll come right up to your room just like Itzy did. That must be it. All your troubles with Loweman must have started then. What did you two do up there in your room," she said smiling mischievously as she turned and walked away?

Thank you, I said to the capricious universe.

I was nearly at my dorm when I realized I hadn't walked her back to Halcion Hall. Finding Browne leaning against the wall when I entered South Hall was disorienting. He looked like he had forgotten where he was going and had come to rest against the wall while attempting to revive his memory. As our eyes met our two stony faces repulsed each other.

I couldn't resist saying something. "Keeping up to date on my activities? We haven't seen each other in a few weeks. Let me know if there are any blanks to fill in." And immediately regretted it, so childishly stupid.

"Dean Loweman asked me to tell you he would like to see you in his office tomorrow afternoon around two."

Would like to see me? Huh! In the afternoon, not three in the morning? Something must be up –my dismissal?

"What for?"

"He didn't say. Just be there at two."

23

AND YOUR NAME, SIR, IS WHAT?

One evening, I was passing by the library for a different reason. A guy leapt out from the darkness of the bushes, ran up to me, calling my name, causing me to turn just in time for him to land a solid punch on my jaw, staggering me sideways and knocking me down.

"Why di'th you 'oo dhat?" I asked with my hand feeling around in my mouth while struggling to regain my footing. "Who are you?" I added as I looked at the blood on my hand.

Having retreated about two arms length away, he shouted, "Don't you go near Betty Lou. She's my girl." He then turned and began to run away.

"Oou broke my tooff," I yelled (hand back in my mouth). "And I had my hand'th in my coa' pocke'th too when you hith me. That'th not fair. And I'm *bleeding*!"

"Then you know I'm serious," reached me from the darkness.

"Who are you anyway?"

Quite clearly, I heard laughing followed by, "Chuck… Willard," as he fled like the Joker after a prank in a Batman story.

It was all so unbelievable. But then, on the other hand, it did seem to have a certain odd fit, in general, with my life as a collection of colliding events.

For example, it so happened that the tooth that broke off was the one I had badly chipped in a diving accident when I was eight. It was the tooth I always tried to hide by smiling with my upper lip inflexibly held down over my upper teeth. I realized ironically; *Now I'll have to do something about it. I'll no longer look demented when I smile! What a relief. I should thank him.*

But then my male hormones cried out, Hey, wait. This is not good. You can't let him get away WITH THAT! But I didn't even know where he lived. I'd never seen him before.

I walked slowly back to South Hall, mulling over the absurdity of what this Chuck person had done, and didn't see anyone until I opened the door to my room halfway down the second-floor hall.

"Gosh!" said Doug. "What happened to you? You're covered with blood."

"Some guy named Chuck Willard hit me in the mouth."

"Chuck who?"

"Willard. Said Betty Lou is his girlfriend."

"That's crazy. I never heard of him. You look terrible. You need to see the nurse."

"I don't think so. It doesn't hurt much. But he broke my tooth off at the gum."

"Did you get him back?"

"I didn't have time. He took right off after he hit me."

"How'd you get his name?"

"Crazy. He yelled it to me as he ran off. I had my hands in my trench coat pockets when he hit me. I couldn't do anything."

"You think you should tell Dean Lowen?"

"No. I can't do that. Besides, I don't want anything to do with Lowen. He'll just figure out a way to make it my fault."

"OK. Then how you gonna' get back at him?"

"I don't know if I should, Doug."

"You're not scared, are you?"

"I'm in so much trouble right now with Dean Lowen. If I get involved in anything he doesn't like, somethin' that draws attention to me, he'll get me chucked out of school."

"Well, something needs to happen. We need to find out where he lives. I can go get him for you."

"No. Please. Don't do anything. Promise? It's my problem. I need to deal with it."

"You should ask Betty? She's got to know about this if she's going out with him. Maybe I could talk to Nancy. She can talk to Betty."

"No, I don't want your girlfriend involved. If Betty Lou brings it up—and remember, it's Betty Lou, Doug. Don't ever slip and call her Betty or Lou. She doesn't like it—if Betty Lou brings it up with Nancy, that's different. I don't even know if she knows about this."

I could tell Doug wanted in on the action, even if he had to make it happen himself. This was beginning to expand in an undesirable way. "Just wait until I can think about this, okay?"

"He's got to pay for the damage at least, Jer."

If it weren't so bizarre, I would have thought how considerate Doug was in trying to come to my aid, especially since I knew he thought of me as a flying saucer space alien. All of a sudden, I was his man, not the loony he lived with. After brief consideration, I concluded it was a natural fit for his straight-arrow personality. No surprise there, just another unwanted layer to the problem.

All right, he was being nice, though I knew he was going to make things worse if I couldn't come up with a plan of action fast.

"I'll see Betty Lou tomorrow and ask what she knows about this guy. Wait until then. Okay, Doug?" As an afterthought, I added, "You know, Doug, I'm not even going out with Betty Lou. I know she must still think I'm crazy for asking her to marry me that time."

"Did you say marry? I thought you said, 'go steady.' You asked Betty to marry you? On your first date?"

What had I done? I just inadvertently added another unpredictable absurd layer to my existence.

The law of unintended consequences had just opened up a branch office in my life.

· · ·

I rarely saw Lou during classes, so I waited the next day until school ended and went to the women's dorm to find her. On the way there, all kinds of things flooded my mind. Did she even know what happened? If not, I'd have to tell her with great care. Was she dating him? Would she think it was my fault? Maybe I should hide my broken tooth. I didn't want her to feel sorry for me before she reacted to Chuck's attack. I didn't think it would go well no matter what or how I explained any of it.

The lobby in the women's dorm was a beehive of girls returning from classes. As a rare male visitor, I attracted attention. Reluctantly, I approached the person on duty at the lobby desk. It was my misfortune to find it was Jane, one of Betty Lou's closest friends. Jane wanted to talk. We did some back and forth, then she asked why I was there. She paged Betty Lou, and a few minutes later, she appeared. Jane pretended to go back to some task. Lou asked what I wanted while I tried to maneuver her out of Jane's hearing range. I suggested we go into the dating room opposite the desk for some privacy. It was called the dating room because couples could meet there in private as long as they left the door wide open with a view of the sofa so everyone could see who was really desperate enough to use the dating room. It was required that you get the Women Dean's permission to use the room.

Upon my insistence, and after glancing over at Jane repeatedly, Betty Lou reluctantly agreed to talk there without the dean's permission. Before Lou arrived in the lobby, I had been arguing and speculating with myself. *She knows about Chuck and me. And she's angry with me. She has no reason to be angry. Why is she angry? Oh. Maybe she doesn't want to talk to me at all. Or she doesn't want anyone to thinks she's dating a bozo by being seen in the dating room, especially by Jane.*

With just a tinge of impatience, she said, "What is it, Jerry?"

Admittedly I was reluctant to start. I lifted my head, looked above her, and said, "Aaaah," as my opening statement.

"Oh, Jerry! What happened to your tooth?"

I'm Not Here

I had forgotten to keep my stiff upper lip stiff.

"Chuck Willard hit me," I blurted out. So much for a slow, subtle approach.

"Chuck-who hit you?"

"Willard. Do you know him?"

"Yes, I do. I met him on a picnic with some other people. I can't believe this. He's such a quiet, calm person. Are you sure it was him?"

"Were you on a date with him on that picnic?"

"No. Not at all. You're sure it was him? What does he look like?"

"I'm not sure, but he told me his name."

"He hit you and then told you his name? That's crazy! When did he hit you?"

"Last night near the library."

"Did he say why?"

"He said you were his girlfriend, and I should stay away from you or else." I added the "or else."

"No! He really said that?"

"Yes. What's going on?"

"I don't know. Nothing's going on. I only saw him that once."

"Do you know where he lives?"

"He lives off-campus. With the Physics Professor and his wife. It was their picnic I went to. He was there too. Why do you want to know?"

"I want to see him."

"What are you thinking of doing?"

"Nothing. But this guy I never saw before jumps out of the bushes, knocks out my front tooth, knocks me to the ground, and as he runs away tells me his name and says to stay away from you. I'd like to at least get a chance to look at him in the light of day."

"You're going to fight him, aren't you?"

"No, no. No fight. No, no, not at all. But that's sort of up to him. It depends. If he tries to hit me again... then I really don't

227

know what I'll need to do." I was trying to give her a definite no without saying no even though I had said no repeatedly. She wasn't convinced. Deep down, I really wanted to hit him.

"Don't you think he should pay to fix my tooth?" After all, I explained, I was the injured party. That earned me some sympathy. She agreed he shouldn't have hit me. But she felt sorry for him too. He was just a poor boy, didn't even have enough money to go to school, he was living with those people, they were sponsoring him, she might talk to him, but she really didn't know him. And on and on we went for maybe another ten minutes. Twelve at the most. Long enough. Too long.

"Why don't you tell Dean Lowman?"

That would only make me look bad, I told her.

"With who," she wanted to know.

I explained with my friends in my dorm, and it would probably become too big of a thing at the school, and I didn't want that attention.

Anyway, I left the dating room feeling I came away with a little part of something. She wasn't dating him and maybe wouldn't in the future, and he lived off-campus. Which meant if I was willing to risk it, I could walk her back to the dorm at night, and it wouldn't be a good idea to try to see Chuck to settle this thing. What I didn't get was an enthusiastic, Yeah! The worm deserves to have his lights punched out. But my inclinations were already beginning to shift. I knew if I went after him, she would not look kindly upon that act, nor me, and there was no likelihood of getting a dime out of him either.

Now I was half as upset and twice as confused. It was another situation where things slid sideways, not forward. As I walked back to my dorm, I realized ironically, all this was taking place on a more visceral level than peace, love, turn the other cheek, Jesus loves you, at WMC, and nobody thought to bring it up. Well, it was another case of side-by-side realities. I knew clearly which one had the upper hand and I planned to, or rather, had no choice but to deal with it.

I'm Not Here

...

"He's up at the library," Doug had just burst into our room out of breath. "He's waiting to walk Betty Lou back to her dorm. We got him surrounded. Come on. It's a chance for you to get him."

"I need to get dressed first, Doug."

"Oh, Yeah. Okay, I'll go ahead," and he bolted for the door. "Don't worry if he tries to get away. We'll stop him.

It had been two days since Chuck had hit me. I still hadn't decided what I should do. Well, now it was out of my hands. I groaned and fell back on my bed. It felt like I was tied down across a railroad track with only seconds before the train reached me. But I wasn't. I got up, got dressed, left the dorm, started for the library, to do what?

As I left South Hall, I saw what appeared to be a pulsating mass at the edge of the campus lawn a hundred yards away. I knew what it was, but I transformed it into the Blob from the hokey sci-fi movie. A gelatinous, quivering form that dissolves its prey by oozing over it. It helped, but that didn't last long. As I got closer to the Blob, the reality of what I needed to do asserted itself. In an attempt to work myself up, I muttered to myself, *Oh, does he ever deserve this. I'm going to pulverize him. How big is he? Doesn't matter. If I don't make a good show of it, I'll never be able to show my face. He's my height. That makes it even. Almost there. There must be eight, ten guys around him. I don't even know some of them. He must be terrified. He really looks small, like a trapped animal. Nearly there!*

The circle parted. "We kept him here Jerry! Just like we promised."

Chuck stood motionless with clenched fists held at his sides.

What do you do in such a situation? Walk right up to the guy and punch him in the mouth? And then what? Ten minutes of a shootout at the O.K. Corral? Was that what this bunch expected? We stood looking at each other without moving.

I began, "You think what you did was such a good idea now, Chuck?

No response.

"You've never even gone out with Betty Lou. Have you? What makes you think she's your girlfriend? You know, there are probably four other guys trying to date her? You planning to punch all of them in the mouth too?"

He didn't respond. And then I knew. I couldn't do anything to him. Poor Chuck. This was so unfair. He looked so scared. Did these guys, acting like bullies, think this was fair? Yes, they did. Where was this screwy sympathy I felt for Chuck coming from?

Why don't I know half of these boys in this ring?

I opened my mouth and hoped something tough-for-the-toughs and something reasonable for Chuck would come out. That's as far as my brain could go. I started up again. I showed him my broken tooth.

"This is what you did. See? For a girl that barely knows you. *Crazy!*" I shouted. "You think Betty Lou is impressed by this?"

Silence.

"We're in college, not grade school, Chuck. This isn't a grammar school playground," which was the last time I had a kind of fight. Then, two eighth-graders held me while a fifth-grade classmate punched me in the stomach because the girl he liked, liked me. As it turned out, I didn't like her. I liked a girl who liked the kid that punched me in the stomach. Some insanities just repeat with slight variations.

I looked around at the circle to see their reaction. Some still had clenched fists and looked like they wanted blood. The rest had puzzled, confused expressions, which might be tipping the situation in his favor and mine too, or not. I glanced around to see if Dean Lowman was coming this way from North Hall to drag me back to his office by my ears, or even worse, Lou getting off from work, walking by.

I'm Not Here

"You don't behave like that in college, Chuck. We're supposed to use our minds to solve our problems. Not our fists. And this is a religious college on top of that. You ever read the words on the archway in front of the main building? It says, Gateway to Service. You know what that means?" I hoped he did, and the others too. I sure didn't.

Right then, I didn't think anyone in the self-righteous mob was in a mood to show any Christian charity to Chuck for what he did or me for what I wasn't doing.

Of course, college and Christianity had nothing to do with this situation, but it sounded good, and had an initial punch to it. And that's what was needed to get Chuck safely away and the vigilantes off my back.

Why compound two acts of stupidity, Chuck's and theirs, with a third one on my part?

I can't pretend that I had any specific awareness of this concept at the time. It was just pure intuition that put those words in my mind.

I checked the group again. Some were nodding in agreement. The adrenaline level was declining. Maybe this was working. I'd have to wait and see how the circular mob reacted afterwards.

Peripherally I saw someone exit the library. Betty Lou. My stomach sank as she turned and walked within twenty feet of us on her way back to her dorm. She did not look at all happy. That was a problem yet to be resolved, I realized, but back to the one at hand.

There was no intention, on my part, to get 'even' any longer. I was really feeling sorry for Chuck. Ash-white, he looked like a drowning man with no land in sight.

I was running out of ideas but knew I had to keep the patter coming fast, at least until Lou was gone. "What have you got to say, Chuck?" He didn't speak. "You want Betty Lou? Ask her out on a date. There she goes. If she wants to go out, fine. Walk her home at night. I will too. But let's let her decide which one she wants to go with just so we don't have to repeat this ridiculousness again. That agreeable with you?"

He nodded slightly.

"You know what, Chuck; I'm not even dating her. She doesn't want to go steady with me or anyone." He looked around at the circle of eight then back at me.

"Just get out of here, Chuck."

The circle parted, he turned and walked away. I wondered if I had seemed cowardly or clever as I turned back to look at the circular firing squad. They all looked at me. No one said anything. They parted again, and I started back to the dorm by myself.

At age nineteen, I was a long way from understanding what was happening or why I did what I did, but one day I suspected that it might be unintended consequences that might lead me to the edge of what is real. Which made my friend Murphy's quip, "don't miss it if you can" profoundly clear. Thank you, Murphy, my old college friend, wherever you are.

Epilogue

These stories have that hope of all youth, that life will find a way forward, and that its purpose is the possibility of true and lasting love. They are and are not exceptional, just as your life is, as all lives are filled with blindsiding lunacy, surprising joy, and unexpected sadness.

I left WMC at the end of that academic year angry and confused. Within a short period of time, I came to realize that neither the powers that be nor I were wrong. We just had different views of reality: theirs' carved in stone, mine just emerging, which put me at a disadvantage. What surfaced over the next few years was the realization that not just their truth, but all truths are fabrications, and that reality is whatever anyone thinks it is. Mine became the life of an artist.

I have come to the conclusion that life doesn't have a resolution, a tidy summing up. Life just goes along from one day to another then ends in the middle of something or other. However, I must confess that I seldom sleep more than five or six hours a night for fear of missing any of it.

About the Author

JERRY VIS spent the earliest years of his life in Paterson, New Jersey, where he was born in 1939 into a blue-collar family struggling to overcome the lingering effects of the Great Depression. He has an M.F.A. in fine art and taught for many years in public school and college. He is also the author of *Paterson Boy: My Family and Other Strangers: A Memoir in Twenty-Eight Stories.*

www.ingramcontent.com/pod-product-compliance
Lightning Source LLC
Chambersburg PA
CBHW071430070526
44578CB00001B/55